Journalists in
PERIL

Media Studies Series

Journalists in PERIL

EDITED BY

Nancy J. Woodhull
Robert W. Snyder

Transaction Publishers
New Brunswick (U.S.A.) and London (U.K.)

Library of Congress Catalog Number: 98-5463
ISBN: 0-7658-0441-7
Printed in the United States of America

Library of Congress Cataloging-in-Publication Data

Journalists in peril / edited by Nancy J. Woodhull and Robert W. Snyder.
   p. cm.
Originally published in the Fall 1996 issue of Media studies journal.
Includes bibliographical references.
ISBN 0-7658-0441-7 (alk. paper)
   1. Freedom of the press. 2. Journalists—Crime against. 3. Crime and
the press. 4. Government and the press. I. Woodhull, Nancy J. II. Snyder,
Robert W., 1955–
PN4736.J68   1998
070.4—dc21   98-5463
                                                             CIP

This book is dedicated to all journalists who
have died in pursuit of their calling.

Contents

"The Balkan media's plight is urgent," reports a member of the board of directors of the Committee to Protect Journalists, after a fact-finding trip to the former Yugoslavia. "Without a free press, the dream of reviving a multiethnic society after years of savage violence will remain just that."

Part III: Government Repression

"What happens when one of the world's most freewheeling and least regulated societies is taken over by one of the most control-minded regimes on earth?" inquires a journalist with long Asian experience. "Clearly, as of July 1, 1997, it will take Herculean efforts to preserve, much less expand, Hong Kong's press freedom."

A China analyst relates the concerns of Hong Kong journalists whose news organizations want to participate in the vast but censored Chinese media market: "Many reporters quite honestly confess that they feel caught in a growing tendency toward self-censorship."

A Russian media analyst evaluates the state of press freedom in his country after the demise of the Soviet system: "The mass media and journalists are caught between the market, with its economic pressures, and the authorities, who try to control them by withholding information, issuing economic threats and pressuring journalists."

"While the sheer magnitude of the mess in Nigeria and the dangerous prospects of defiant publishing make an absolute victory impossible," writes an exiled Nigerian editor, "the press has no choice but to continue to push the government to keep clear in its mind that the age of guns and jackboots, having become absolutely anachronistic, will soon pass."

"Can a nation that has tasted freedom of the press be forced back into censorship and the imprisonment of independent journalists? Indonesia may well offer an answer," writes an analyst of Asian press freedom.

"Britain no longer rules the waves," argues a London barrister and expert in Commonwealth law, "but in countries throughout the world it is the British rule book that tends to be waved at journalists and authors, in an edition much more strict than applies in Britain."

"While their colleagues around the world face harassment from thugs, physical attacks, assassinations, extralegal pressure from police and outright censorship," notes an Ankara reporter writing under a pseudonym, "Turkish journalists are intimidated and censored under laws that, at first glance, seem friendly to press freedom."

Part IV: Civil Unrest

"In Algeria, a crazy slaughter has set the country on fire," writes an exile living in France. "Journalists are among this dirty war's casualties—59 of them as of August 1996. As the only witnesses of this underreported warfare, theirs is a highly perilous trade. They are caught between an oppressive government and murderous armed Islamic groups."

"Over the last decade, 10 immigrant journalists have been murdered in the United States of America," notes an investigative reporter. "In a country where it is widely assumed that reporters are safe from violence, their deaths are a reminder that the protections of the First Amendment are imperfectly applied, that mainstream reporters are generally much safer than their immigrant counterparts and that the tendency to put immigrant journalists in a separate category leaves them in dangerous isolation."

Part V: Organized Crime

"It is impossible to provide an armed escort for every journalist," writes an Italian reporter who has covered organized crime for many years. "The only way to make reporters safe is to eliminate the Mafia threat. And that will happen only through mobilized citizens and a mobilized judiciary."

The slain Irish investigative reporter is commemorated in her own words and the words of her former editor: "She was a brave and brilliant reporter."

Part VI: Portfolio

Photographs from wars and civil disorders reveal a fundamental truth about photography: "If photographers are close enough to shoot their pictures, they are more than close enough to get shot."

Part VII: Solutions

"Violence against journalists in the United States declined dramatically when journalism professionalized in the early 20th century," writes a historian of violence against the press. "But they will never be entirely safe. In an age with any political action at all, good journalists should expect some friction."

"Journalists can be wounded, often seriously, even without being in the proverbial line of fire," reflects the managing editor of the Daily Oklahoman. "Those of us who direct coverage owe them a chance to be made whole again."

News organizations themselves must take responsibility for safeguarding their staffers, argues the director of The Freedom Forum European Center: "One killer, be it a mobster or trigger-happy soldier, brought to justice for murdering a journalist sends a signal that it is no longer open season on reporters and camera men and women."

Part VIII: Interviews

Reflections from W.C. Heinz, World War II correspondent for the New York Sun, with New York free-lancer George Robinson.

Kemal Kurspahic is former editor of the Sarajevo daily *Oslobodjenje*.

Bob Greene is professor of journalism at Hofstra University and a former investigative reporter.

Maria Caballero is special investigations editor/national editor of *Cambio 16*, Colombia.

Donna Ferrato is a photojournalist and is founder and co-chair of Domestic Abuse Awareness Project.

Part IX: Review Essay

"George Polk was a troublemaker, and in that sense he was an embodiment of the best traditions of his profession," concludes a journalist who reviews three accounts of Polk's murder and its aftermath. "As long as his story inspires one or two journalists to resist—to continue to make trouble—then George Polk will not have died in vain."

Preface

When you look at The Freedom Forum Journalists Memorial in Arlington, Va., you see two things: the names of hundreds of journalists who died on assignment or were murdered for what they wrote, photographed or broadcast—and your own reflection.

For a journalist, that prompts an almost unavoidable thought: It could have been me.

Those who died may have had more courage or less luck than other reporters, producers, photographers and camera operators. But they died because they were practicing a craft that many thousands more practice in safety.

If not in the memory of the dead, then at least in their own self-interest, journalists have an obligation to protect one another. To stand up for one another. To recognize that an injury to one is an injury to all.

The stories of threats to journalists contained in this book carry many different lessons, but this one runs through all of them: The people who would intimidate or kill journalists are usually terrified that someone might find out. Journalists who want to protect one another need do nothing more than what should come naturally to them: report on threats to journalists—big threats and small threats, whether they are directed against the international luminaries of the profession or small timers.

The second lesson of this volume applies to all the people who look at the memorial who are not journalists. Because the reflection they see is also a big part of the fight to protect journalists.

Next to tough and timely reporting that establishes the facts of a case, nothing protects a journalist so much as public outrage and public support. Ordinary citizens, wherever they are, have an enormous role to play in pressuring the thugs and tyrants who would like to stifle the freedom of the press.

Coal miners, another group of people who do dangerous work, used to carry canaries into the mines: If a bird died, it was a sign of bad air that would soon kill the miners.

In democracies and countries that would like to be democracies, the journalist is like a canary in a mineshaft. To kill a journalist, to imprison a journalist or to threaten a journalist is to attack the people who are responsible for conducting the conversation of democracy. And once journalists are in danger, everyone else is not far behind.

The Freedom Forum Journalists Memorial is located in Freedom Park, a place in Arlington, Va., that celebrates the spirit of freedom and the struggle to preserve freedom. Near the memorial are icons of free- dom—segments of the Berlin Wall, a bronze casting of a ballot box used in the first South African elections open to black voters, banners seeking women's right to vote and more. The juxtaposition of the me- morial and the icons are a reminder that the freedom of journalists is tied to the freedom of all people.

As of the summer of 1998, there will be 1,563 names on the memo- rial—and room for many more. Every year, additional names will be added as journalists die in the line of duty. It would be naive to think that the list of names on the memorial will stop growing anytime soon. But it would be craven to sit back and watch the list grow without doing anything about it. That is why the work of The Freedom Forum, the Committee to Protect Journalists and all the other organizations and individuals in this fight matters so very much.

The Freedom Forum has and will focus on international programs illuminating the dangers that journalists face. Under the heading "Jour- nalists Under Fire: Media Under Siege," meetings in Hong Kong, Lon- don, Dublin, Buenos Aires, Capetown, Johannesburg, Arlington, Va., and New York City bring together journalists and people who care about journalists. Together, the participants explore the threats that reporters face around the world—and the best ways to fight back.

The act of reporting, for which so many people have given their lives, is grounded in the belief that when people know something, they can make a difference. And that is as true for the protection of journal- ists as it is for any other cause.

When we keep faith with the names on the memorial—and, sadly, the many more that are going to be placed there—we do more than honor those who have died. We also protect each other and safeguard the democracy that all of us share or hope to share.

—The Editors

Part I
Overview

1

The Meaning of the Murders

William A. Orme Jr.

Djilali Arabidou was one of Algeria's best-known photojournalists. The weekly newsmagazine where he worked, *Algeria-Actualité,* was known to be editorially sympathetic to the military government and its war against Islamist insurgents. In March 1996, in a quiet residential district outside Algiers, Arabidou was intercepted and shot dead by rebel gunmen.

Later that month, villagers in Chechnya discovered the blindfolded body of Nadezdha Chaikova, a correspondent for the Moscow weekly *Obshchaya Gazeta,* who was known for her hard-hitting coverage of Russian military atrocities. Chaikova had been beaten and executed with a bullet to the back of her head.

In May, Parag Kumar Das, the editor in chief of the largest newspaper in the Indian state of Assam, was picking his son up from school when gunmen opened fire from a passing car. His death was widely seen as a reprisal for his editorial advocacy of Assamese secession and denunciations of human rights violations by state security agencies.

Investigative reporter Veronica Guerin was driving near her North Dublin home in late June. When she stopped at a traffic light a motorcycle pulled alongside her, and a gunman on the back took aim. She was shot five times and died as the motorcycle sped off. An outraged Irish public immediately assumed that her killing had been ordered by one of the powerful local crime bosses whose rackets she had exposed.

In July, Kutlu Adali, a Turkish Cypriot newspaper columnist who had urged peaceful accommodation with the island's ethnic Greek majority, was shot dead near his home by the self-styled Turkish Revenge Brigade. The shadowy far-right terror faction had earlier vowed to "punish" all those it deemed unfaithful to the Turkish nationalist cause.

3

Arabidou, Chaikova, Das, Guerin and Adali worked in vastly different environments, with varied professional responsibilities and contrasting reporting styles. But they are now all linked as five of the 26 journalists slain in political assassinations in the first eight months of 1996.

These killings were tragically typical of the violent deaths the Committee to Protect Journalists (CPJ) has documented over the years. The murdered journalists were local reporters, not foreign correspondents. They were not casualties of the battlefield or victims of fatal accidents or random acts of violence. They were all killed in cold blood by assassins who knew exactly who they were, and whose unambiguous intent was to silence a critical voice or put a stop to independent reporting.

There is another common factor in these and the other murders confirmed by CPJ in 1996: No suspects have been officially identified, much less arrested and prosecuted.

The seeming inability or unwillingness of national authorities to find and punish those responsible for these deaths is not in itself an indictment of a political system. Contract murders and political assassinations are notoriously hard to solve even in peaceful, developed democracies. Despite a recently revived investigative effort, the U.S. Justice Department has still failed to arrest any serious suspects in five different but possibly related murders of Vietnamese-American journalists stretching back more than a decade.

Veronica Guerin's murder, though without precedent in the British Isles, is another case in point. In response to the intense public outrage at her killing and the resulting political pressure on the government to do something about it, the Republic of Ireland's national police force embarked on one of the biggest investigative efforts in its history. In addition, Guerin's employer at the *Sunday Independent,* publishing baron Tony O'Reilly, has offered to pay 100,000 Irish pounds—about $160,000—for information leading to arrest and prosecution of the killers. No arrests had been made as of when the journal went to press, however. And Ireland's strict libel laws and evidentiary procedures prevented the police (and therefore journalists as well) from naming as a suspect the crime boss believed by investigators to have ordered the murder.

But in most of the murders of journalists that CPJ has closely examined, there was never ever any serious, sustained attempt to identify and punish those responsible, and little political pressure on authorities to do so. Even when local or national authorities clearly had no prior knowledge of or involvement in the crime, it is sometimes in their real or presumed political interest to let local journalists operate in an atmosphere of fear and intimidation.

The perception that officials are less than vigorous in their investigations into crimes against journalists only fuels suspicion, fairly or not, of links between the murderers and local political interests or state security forces. Cynicism about such cases can transmute quickly into real fear. Whatever their intentions, the failure of authorities to vigorously and visibly respond to these politically motivated murders intimidates reporters and inhibits the development of a free press.

In Algeria and Chechnya, where thousands of civilians have died, the failure to mount a serious investigation into the death of a reporter is an arguably understandable consequence of the chaos of civil war. Yet the failure of Algerian authorities to arrest and charge even a single individual in connection with any of the 59 murders of journalists there for three years calls into question their interest in combating this reign of terror. The Algerian government has benefited, both internationally and domestically, from the justified opprobrium directed at the journalists' assassins, as well as from the understandable tendency of many previously democratically minded Algerian journalists to accept the military regime as the lesser of two evils. (Some experienced observers are convinced that several of these apparent Islamist murders have been carried out for propaganda reasons by state security forces. These suspicions have not been allayed by the government's inability or unwillingness to mount investigations.)

And in Chechnya, the Chaikova homicide is just one of five known deliberate murders of reporters covering the war there, out of a total of 10 documented deaths of reporters through August of 1996. (There are undoubtedly more: At least four other reporters are missing and feared dead). Making the trend even more disturbing, two of those five murders—both unpunished to date—were by uniformed Russian soldiers at official army checkpoints. Given the Yeltsin government's inability or unwillingness to take a hard investigative look into the murders of eight journalists elsewhere in the Russian Federation over the past two years, Russian reporters say they now operate under the assumption that there is official tolerance for and perhaps even active complicity in such crimes.

Every year the Committee to Protect Journalists releases its carefully documented list of journalists who have been killed "in the line of duty," to use the shopworn police department phrase. This includes not just murder victims, but also journalists who have died while dispatched on dangerous assignments. Reporters always ask if things are getting better or worse. The figures alone do not tell the story. There were no deaths from combat cross fire in the first half of 1996, for example, a stark departure from the previous five years. But that is a result of the cease-fire in Bosnia, not an indication of diminishing dangers for journalists on post-Cold War battlefields. Six journalists were murdered in Russia since January, a shocking statistic for a country that hadn't registered a single such assassination five years ago. But would anyone seriously contend that Russian journalism is more controlled or intimidated today than it was under the Soviet Union? Paradoxically, the deaths of journalists are as much a testament to the emergence of a free press as they are a gauge of the limits of press freedom.

Between 1986 and 1995 CPJ documented 453 violent deaths of journalists killed on assignment (in an accident or in a cross fire) or in apparent reprisal for their reporting or media affiliation. The great majority of these cases fell into the latter category. As in 26 of the 27 deaths documented through August 1996, these were victims of assassination.

Covering combat is inherently dangerous, but even in Bosnia, Somalia and Chechnya the deaths of journalists are often the result of seemingly deliberate executions of clearly identified reporters by armed combatants. These incidents are often impossible to prove definitively— was the sniper aiming at that cameraman, or just out to kill anything that moved?—but reporters covering these conflicts feel less and less protected by their theoretically recognized status as noncombatants. Rebel gunmen at combat-zone checkpoints are rarely versed in the fine points of the Geneva Convention.

Increasingly, insurgent factions in multilateral conflicts appear to see Western journalists as integral—and uniquely visible and vulnerable— components of the international military and political forces arrayed against them. For a Bosnian Serb sniper or a Somali machine gunner working the back of a warlord's "technical," the foreign press was at least as legitimate a target as their local ethnic or political enemies.

An examination of the past decade's figures reveals several overlapping trends, some extremely disturbing and others quite encouraging.

When CPJ was founded in 1981, the most dangerous area of the world for working journalists was Latin America. We now know of nearly 100 documented cases of state-sponsored killings of journalists in the late 1970s and early 1980s in Argentina alone. Army-linked death squads also murdered scores of reporters in El Salvador and Guatemala in that period. With few exceptions, the victims in Central

America and the Southern Cone were local, and the motivation explicitly ideological.

Now state-sponsored violence against Latin American journalists is extremely rare, and its decline corresponds directly to the replacement of military regimes by increasingly stable electoral democracies with lively, independent news media. (The real physical danger to journalists in Latin America today comes from criminal forces, who, though often in league with state security agencies, do not represent the same kind of institutional threat to journalists and press freedom in the region.)

Globally, however, the homicide rate among journalists should not be misread as a kind of inverse press freedom index. In the most repressive societies, murders of journalists are extremely rare because journalists themselves are extremely rare. In the past decade CPJ has not had a single confirmed killing of a working reporter in North Korea, Saudi Arabia, Cuba, Libya, Syria or Myanmar. This is hardly an indicator of press freedom.

Conversely, in countries with a large and aggressive press corps, there are abundant motives and opportunities for violent attacks on journalists. Examples include India, where 16 reporters were killed in the past 10 years, and Brazil, where 10 were murdered. And there are many countries, such as China and Ethiopia, where journalists are rarely killed but are routinely imprisoned for long terms under gruelingly harsh conditions.

Societies that have only recently emerged from autocratic or totalitarian rule—places as culturally and politically diverse as Russia, Cambodia and Peru—are the real press freedom battlegrounds today. These are political systems that let independent publications circulate freely, but that rarely investigate—much less prosecute—violent attacks against reporters and editors and publishers.

Even when journalists are targeted by the government's declared enemies—armed separatists, nationalist zealots, drug traffickers—the chilling effect of the attacks may be welcomed by those with the power to combat them. A frightened reporter is rarely an aggressive reporter.

A detailed look at the murder of journalists over the past decade also sheds disturbing light on the varying pathologies of countries that have succumbed to criminal violence or civil war. Algeria, the most extreme case with 59 journalists killed from May 1993 to August 1996, is unique in scale but not in kind. Reporters and editors of the "secular" press are increasingly targeted for harassment and worse by fundamentalist insurgents throughout the Islamic world.

The former Yugoslavia, in aggregate, had the second largest number of press casualties in the past 10 years with 45 documented deaths. That grim statistic would surprise no observer of the Balkans carnage. Again, however, most of these deaths were not accidental. And most of the victims were local journalists, not foreign correspondents. Most appear to have been personally targeted, both because of their ethnicity and their profession. As in Rwanda, local journalists were singled out in the early stages of genocidal attacks because of their local prominence and influence.

Colombia, with 42 confirmed cases, had the third largest number of documented deaths over the past decade. Most were apparent drug-cartel contract murders. This is certainly an underestimate. Many reported murders of provincial print and radio reporters in Colombia simply could not be confirmed, an endemic problem for a country with the world's highest reported homicide rate. Most of these murders remain not only unsolved but uninvestigated. So inured is the Colombian press to these killings—and so intimidated are many local publishers—that these cases rarely make the front page, if they are indeed covered at all.

The Colombian plague has spread to its immediate neighbors: Journalists from Central America to the southern Andes say coverage of narcotics corruption is now a riskier enterprise than reporting about leftist insurgencies or human rights abuses. That is saying a great deal in countries where the penalty for aggressive political reporting in the past has often been assassination.

Criminal gangs are also targeting journalists in Russia, Central Europe, Central Asia and Indochina. The only murder in memory of a New York City journalist—that of Manuel de Dios Unanue—was a contract hit ordered by the Cali cocaine cartel. As of press time, we don't know if Veronica Guerin's murder had international implications. But we do know that her presumed murderers are the local partners of transnational drug barons who consider the murder of a reporter an appropriate response to unwelcome publicity. In the coming decade, threats to journalism from organized crime are likely to become an even more deadly problem than political persecution.

In Asia, where leaders of both the left and right proclaim that press freedom is inimical to indigenous "values," the dangers faced by journalists are typically imprisonment or legal harassment. The murders of journalists, in proportion to the size of the working press, are relatively rare. This may be more of an indication of the caution exercised by the Asian press than of the restraint or broad-mindedness of the region's rulers.

In both the Philippines and Tajikistan, CPJ has confirmed 29 violent job-related deaths of journalists over the past decade, almost all of them apparently deliberate, politically motivated murders. Politically and culturally, however, these two countries are atypical of Asia.

The Philippines, marked by a legacy of Spanish colonialism and U.S. military rule, has a history and social structure arguably more akin to Latin America than to Asia. The pattern of unprosecuted murders of provincial Filipino journalists who uncovered corruption and human rights abuses by local landowners and security chiefs is disturbingly similar to death-squad killings of reporters in Central and South America. (Though common in the Marcos era, these homicides continued under the Aquino and Ramos governments—in part, it seems, because local publications were emboldened by the restoration of democracy to touch subjects they would have avoided in the past. Another common denominator with Latin America is a continuing counterinsurgency campaign against Marxist rebels, which has also claimed casualties in the press corps.)

The case of Tajikistan is more distinctive still. Though geographically Asian, this neighbor of China and Afghanistan has never been part of the continent politically. Nominally independent since 1991, Tajikistan remains firmly within Moscow's shrinking sphere of influence. A CPJ investigation demonstrated compelling circumstantial evidence of government complicity in most of the 29 murders of Tajik journalists that we documented since May 1992. Though the government in Dushanbe is wholly dependent on Russian economic and military support, Moscow is rarely taken to task for sustaining a regime that has ruthlessly eliminated all traces of an independent press. The Tajik government resolutely refuses to undertake even cursory investigations into these killings.

The pattern has been consistent over the past 10 years: Somewhere in the world virtually every week a reporter or editor or broadcaster dies a violent death. Still, by any objective global standard, this does not make journalism a particularly hazardous profession. New York taxi drivers have been murdered at nearly the same rate in recent years. Many other professions are statistically more dangerous. Most journalists face no more danger in their working lives than any other ordinary urbanite.

Cynics eyeing the news business from afar could be forgiven for suspecting that accounts of these deaths would not be carried if the victims were, say, firefighters, and not the colleagues (and perhaps the friends) of the journalists writing about them. In most cases they would be right—but not because of collegial favoritism.

A reporter's murder is in itself an important news story if, as is usually the case, the intent of the murderers was to suppress criticism or information. Whether the report comes from a news organization or a press freedom group, it is essential that we as journalists avoid the implication that we believe that the murder of a reporter is inherently more tragic or significant than the killing of any other innocent victim.

When a journalist is slain, it is the political context of the crime that counts. Reports of these deaths do not always make that context clear, but the salient facts are that homicide is the leading cause of job-related deaths for journalists and that such killings take place disproportionately in countries or communities where an independent press is just beginning to take root.

Tragic as they are, the murders of journalists around the world are the by-product of the growth of an independent press around the world. For most of the world, press freedom is an achievement of the late 20th century, the result (and often the catalyst) of democratic revolutions that ended both Soviet communism and military rule by the anti-communist right. The sudden emergence of aggressive, independent news media in such societies is almost invariably resented and combated by authoritarian forces who are losing power and also by new, ostensibly democratic leaders who owe their positions in good part to the power of the press.

These newly won freedoms are fiercely resisted. Even in the more successful emerging democracies, criminal libel suits and huge civil claims are filed by officials and their friends in an effort to frustrate coverage of corruption and human rights abuses. In many countries intimidation is more direct.

But the real story, from West Africa to Central America to East Asia and the former Soviet Union, is that the press keeps fighting back—despite the killings, despite the constant harassment and intimidation. The lengthening honor roll of journalists who have sacrificed their lives in the defense of press freedom should not obscure their lasting achievement: the continuing gains for journalists and journalism on every continent. The numbers of independent reporters and news organizations working around the world have probably doubled in the past decade. Repression often works in the short run: Murder threats are a very effective form of censorship, as any Algerian editorial writer will attest.

But from Moscow to Soweto, from Santiago to Seoul, millions of people are getting uncensored information about politics and economics and their own national cultures for the first time.

Journalists will continue to face violent reprisals from state security forces, from international drug gangs, from armed dissidents of diverse ideological stripes. Yet the stunning global expansion of independent news outlets and new telecommunications links means that most of these threats will be reported and denounced. In more and more places, the good guys are winning, and their stories are getting out.

William A. Orme Jr. is executive director of the Committee to Protect Journalists.

Part II

Reporting from War Zones

2

No Sense at All

Martha A. Teichner

Our crew had set up for my on-camera about Yugoslav Army planes strafing Ljubljana Airport when we saw it: the eruption of black smoke, the licks of flame dancing out of what looked like burning tires in the middle of the shell-pocked runway.

From maybe 200 yards away, we watched as a fire truck raced out onto the tarmac, was forced back by the guns hidden in the woods beyond, tried again and then gave up. The cameraman casually shot the whole thing. Only later did we learn what we had actually seen.

Afterwards, on the long drive back to Zagreb, navigating Slovenian and Croatian checkpoints, he and the sound man wondered aloud to the producer what might have happened to the two young journalists we had met at the airport. They had driven 13 hours overnight to get there, taking endless detours around roadblocks. When they arrived in Ljubljana, they could barely stay awake.

Sizing up their eager determination, the cameraman pointed to the runway and warned them: "Don't take your Jeep out there. It looks like a military vehicle." Minutes before, when we had been out on the runway photographing the damage ourselves, the unmistakable sound of a tank powering up spooked us. We were clearly civilians in our big Volvo and nothing happened to us, but we didn't stick around to push our luck. The cameraman and producer had been covering wars for more than 20 years; the soundman and I, for 15.

We never got to speak further because suddenly, the airport buildings around us were reverberating with gunfire. My crew and I ran and ducked for cover. When the firing died down, we got in our car and sped off to the far perimeter of the airport for the on-camera.

When we got to Zagreb, the wire copy said that two free-lance journalists had been killed by a tank shell at the airport just about the time
we were there. Austrians—young, just out of school—they were among
the first journalists to die in the wars surrounding the break-up of
Yugoslavia.

We reread the story and decided it must be wrong. Then we began to
think about the smoke and flame on the runway, the fire truck, the clank-
ing and rumbling in the woods—it all fit together.

The worst part of what we had witnessed and videotaped was knowing that the two dead Austrians, boys really, had ignored our warning.
They didn't know enough to take it seriously. Their deaths were truly
tragic. Two lives wasted. They should have been learning to be journalists, not playing at covering a war. They died before they could com-
prehend that war is not a game.

It's easy to dismiss the Austrians. They shouldn't have been anywhere near that airport. They had no idea what they were doing. In fact,
there is no difference between them and the American television reporters and camera crews from local affiliates who are sent off to Bosnia
or Somalia or the hotspot *du jour* because the hometown National Guard
unit is there or because their station considers it a great way to boost
ratings during sweeps.

More and more, crews from local affiliates are going to dangerous
places—partly because technology has made it easier and partly, I think,
because local news tends to be more sensational than ever before.

And war *is* sensational. The people most at risk are the television news
teams and still photographers who have to be where the fighting is because that is where the pictures are. Print reporters do not need to take as
many risks because they have safer means of verifying information.

Before some local reporter says nobody could be as stupid as the
Austrians, consider this: I was sent to Beirut in 1983 immediately after
the U.S. Marine barracks was blown up by a suicide car bomber. Several hundred Marines were killed or injured. The attack was possible
because security around the base had been lax. After the fact, sandbag
bunkers were built, big concrete barriers installed, and access became
very, very limited. You could be the best-known TV anchorman in the
United States, but if your name hadn't been left at the entrance, cleared
by Public Affairs, you didn't get in. Guards had orders to shoot at any
unauthorized person or vehicle attempting to crash the gate.

A local reporter and crew from a CBS affiliate, a good-sized station
in a substantial market, arrived in Beirut and requested a Lebanese

driver/translator from our network bureau. I was there when the producer in charge of the office at the time told them: "No heroics. If the driver says don't go someplace, *don't.*" That was the same advice we all followed anywhere there was shelling.

It never occurred to any of us that the people from the affiliate could get in trouble with U.S. forces but they did. Although we had told them what to do to get into the Marine base, they decided just to go there and take their chances. What happened then became the problem of the entire CBS bureau. It wasn't hard to piece together the details because the incident was the talk of the bureau for weeks.

The affiliate crew said they didn't have time to sit and wait for permission. Of course, they were stopped at the gate. Trying to talk their way in didn't work.

If I recall, neither the reporter nor the crew had covered a story overseas before. Certainly they had never faced American soldiers confronting them at gunpoint. They were furious. Who were these goons treating their own countrymen like this? What right did they have to bully the PRESS? Instead of quietly going away and doing what everybody else did to get in, no matter how tedious, they ordered their driver to run the barricade. He refused, so one of the journalists grabbed the wheel. The soldiers opened fire. Nobody was killed, but the driver and one of the guys from the affiliate were shot.

When it's dangerous, and you don't know what's around the next corner, and you don't speak the language, it's not just stupidity that can get you killed. Ignorance can too. So can panic. So can chance.

During the Romanian revolution that overthrew the Ceaucescus in 1989, one member of a French television team was killed when a tank backed over him. I don't remember the nationality of the television reporter who was shot and killed by a sniper in the same public square. He was doing a stand-up at night. His photographer turned on the camera light, making him the perfect illuminated target.

On Christmas night, after the Ceaucescus had been assassinated, CBS News correspondent Bob Simon and I, accompanied by four other CBS people plus our Romanian driver, took the subway to Romanian Television in Bucharest to feed our stories. The subway was the only safe way to travel after sundown. We were escorted out of the station toward the entrance of the television complex holding our passports over our heads, shouting, "American, American," as we had been instructed to do. The jittery soldiers at the gate opened fire on us anyway. Fortunately, they missed.

For the next 11 hours we were held in the freezing cold, at times with guns to our heads. We watched the guards shoot a man who had been startled and had run from the building when huge sheets of broken glass fell from an upper floor. We did everything right and took no unnecessary risks, but we were almost killed.

In a dozen years overseas covering wars, I don't recall an affiliate reporter or crew ever arriving in a war zone with any idea of what to ask their network contacts about how to stay alive. Instead, they ask what they would ask back home—questions about the logistics of cutting and feeding their pieces, questions about live shots and stand-ups, questions about how to get in and out fast because of budget limitations.

I wish I could count the number of times I've seen women reporters from local stations show up wearing their dressed-for-success suits and little flimsy shoes, not the functional, less telegenic garb that is appropriate if you're running for your life.

How many local crews would know or even think to find out that in Bosnia the license plate on their rental car could be a death warrant. Drive up to a Muslim or Croat checkpoint with a Serb plate and you could be shot. For this reason network crews brought cars in from Austria or Hungary, anywhere outside the former Yugoslavia. They also learned that anyplace outside of Belgrade, they had to carry 40 gallon tanks of gas and their own food and water.

Please, leave war coverage to people who do it for a living. God knows it's dangerous enough even for them. Of course there is pressure to get a big story, one with top-notch bang-bang, but experienced reporters take calculated, not foolish, risks. They recognize what they have to gain and what they have to lose. If there is any rule breaking to be done to get a story, let veterans who know what is at stake do it.

A simple but profound lesson that I learned when I began to cover wars is that you only die once. Having war experience is no guarantee that a network correspondent, producer or technician will not get killed, but it is something of an insurance policy. A network reporter who's never been to war before learns from seasoned crews, has a chance to develop instincts, can usually rely on fixers and drivers and translators and local journalists for support. Reporters and crews from affiliates can be like the blind leading the blind, a danger to themselves and other people around them. They are not necessarily local heroes.

According to the Committee to Protect Journalists, 50 members of the press are killed each year, and the job is getting more hazardous. The Freedom Forum recently erected a memorial in Arlington, Va., to journalists worldwide who have lost their lives covering the news. It is a two-story spiral of glass panels with 934 names on it. What struck those assembled at its unveiling was the amount of blank space left for names to be added.

I wonder how many of the names that will one day appear on those glass panels will be those of people who never should have been sent to war in the first place. I would not like to be the news director or general manager of a local television station, knowing I had sent even one of them off to die.

Martha A. Teichner is a correspondent for CBS News' "Sunday Morning."

3

The Clash of Arms in Exotic Locales

Peter Arnett

It's mid-summer and I'm in Grozny, an appropriate place to write about my scariest moments. The Chechen capital is a volatile brew of late 20th-century geopolitical mayhem—a combination of Sarajevo under siege, the maniacal Beirut of the early 1980s and the last days of Saigon.

Forget much of what you learned about journalistic impartiality when you enter the blackened debris of Grozny: You play by local rules. That means lending your satellite phones to the vodka-swigging Russian soldiers at the checkpoints so they can call their wives or their distant headquarters. So far, no journalist with a satellite phone has been shot in the back after being waved through the checkpoint—more than can be said for some local reporters. And you give lifts to the armed Chechen rebels materializing from the underbrush along country roads. No point in trying to outrun a B-40 rocket, even in an armored car.

Once upon a time, war correspondents were accorded some support and privileges by the armies they covered. Now it's the other way around.

One of the hardest, and most frequent, questions I've had to answer from interviewers and the public is why I willingly travel to places like Chechnya, where being scared comes with the territory. The average Joe equates fear with flight, or as Walter Cronkite, in advising me to flee Baghdad during an on-air discussion on the eve of the Gulf War, said, "Why, you know, save your skin, boy."

I have great regard for Walter Cronkite and my skin. But I have more esteem for the traditions of aggressive international reporting that originated during the mid-19th-century Crimean War and became of great personal motivation to me while I was cutting my journalistic teeth on the Vietnam War. Over a lifetime of practicing what I preach I've rarely had occasion to regret my commitment because fate has spared me injury. I've known many fine colleagues who were not so lucky, and it's with a nod to their memory that I set off on assignments like Chechnya.

In short, I believe that the armpits of the world have to be covered no matter how dangerous they are, because it's important to know what's going on there. And yes, I love a good story, and what is more dramatic than the clash of arms in exotic locales?

I began my career in the simpler times of the Vietnam War, when correspondents covered only their own side, consigning the enemy to the darker places of hell and not, as we do now, routinely crossing the lines to get the other side of the story. In Vietnam we could get as close to the action as we wanted, and in the thrill of the action had to be reminded that the whole point of covering war was to get the news and pictures back, and not play soldiers ourselves.

But it was tempting to play soldier. In the early years I carried a large revolver that I lovingly polished while relishing the approval of the GIs I was covering. I never did fire that pistol at anything other than a beer can and eventually threw it away while running for dear life to board a military transport plane hurriedly departing the Khe Sanh combat base during a Vietcong rocket attack.

Covering Vietnam well was a matter of guts because there was no censorship and most combat units welcomed the press. Such open coverage created unique opportunities for reporters. Yet you lived with the fear of dying a brutal death and tested your resolve constantly by clambering aboard the lead chopper assault ships, leaping out with the point infantry companies and slogging through the boonies with them in monsoon rains and blistering heat until the sudden, bloody encounters with the enemy side gave you the graphic details and vivid pictures for a story.

Sometimes painfully vivid: I was standing next to an American battalion commander in War Zone C northwest of Saigon one morning. As we checked his map, a VC sniper pumped four bullets into his chest. He collapsed in a bloody, dying heap at my feet, yet he tried to spurn my assistance, urging me to run away and save myself. In Vietnam, I saw so many men die bravely that I cannot bear to do otherwise myself.

The tragedy of Vietnam was that Americans and South Vietnamese were dying bravely for a lost cause, a reality brought home daily by the truth of war reporting that contrasted with Washington's upbeat assessments. So in addition to the hazards of the battlefield, there were political pressures applied to our bosses to force us reporters to "get on the team." For some of us there was special scrutiny from the FBI and the CIA. Caught between the truth that we saw and the nation's sense of patriotism, the Vietnam reporters became something like outcasts, destined to defend their professionalism for the rest of their lives.

When the Vietnam War ended I realized that covering conflicts was what I wanted to do with the rest of my life. And I figured I was well prepared for whatever lay ahead because the echoes of Vietnam and its controversies reverberated in every continent, with revolutionary groups and ethnic separatists bidding to achieve their goals violently. But in Central America I was to learn that the media would play a much more sensitive role in the course of events than had previously been the case, and we would consequently face new, frightening pressures from authoritarian governments anxious to conceal their brutalities from the world.

In Vietnam I had taken my chances on the battlefield, knowing that the political pressures from Washington could be reasonably contained by the solid support of AP executives in New York City. But in El Salvador and Guatemala, where negative reporting directly threatened American aid monies, the military governments blatantly attempted to intimidate reporters by laying out death-squad victims in front of our hotels as ghoulish warnings to us to be less critical. Or they leaked hit lists of targeted reporters in attempts, sometimes successfully, to frighten us out of the country. One morning, a four-man Dutch television crew ended up dead, gunned down in El Salvador, and the hundred or so of us reporters there screamed to high heaven to the authorities, hoping that in unity we might stay their hand.

Unfortunately, the Central American style of intimidation has spread across the developing world. So too, fortunately, has the sense of media unity, giving birth to both the influential Committee to Protect Journalists and The Freedom Forum, amongst others, all dedicated to defending the principle of press freedom and supporting embattled reporters.

But unity is for the larger issues. Each day we have to fight our individual competitive battles for the story, a particularly challenging task in television news, where the video camera is often a target of angry mobs and vengeful thugs.

The safety of the news team is always uppermost in my mind on CNN assignments, but so too is the need for enough video to carry the story. One technique I used in Moscow in the waning days of the Cold War, covering the regular demonstrations of Jewish *refuseniks,* was to gather the producer, the sound man and me around the cameraman in a giant bear hug. Locked together, for a minute or two we could withstand the inevitable assault from KGB thugs and shoot a few pictures before we all went crashing to the ground.

In Bosnia, the rising toll of journalist deaths persuaded major news organizations to invest in expensive, distinctive white-painted armored vehicles that clamored through the streets of sniper-wracked Sarajevo with their cargoes of flak-vested, helmeted, sweating news hounds. The life-saving "hard cars" are routinely showing up now wherever bullets fly.

As the information age and its portable communications technology transform the world, the old "whose side are you on" accusation once hurled at the reporters of the Vietnam War is becoming increasingly irrelevant. Today we're on everyone's side, or no one's, depending on your point of view. There is a widespread belief that all participants in a conflict have a right to express themselves. A reporter, then, is obligated to go as far as it takes to unearth all sides of a story—provided that the reporter gets to ask plenty of questions and judge the answers independently. That's where the professionalism comes in. The once gung ho war correspondent has become a diplomat and educator in addition to a reporter.

During the Gulf War bombing of Baghdad, I was the subject of a bitter national debate about whether I should be reporting from the Iraqi side at all. Critics argued that I was dispensing only information supportive of Saddam Hussein and was therefore threatening the success of the coalition effort. Other critics suggested that live war coverage should be banned in future conflicts because it imperiled national security.

The truth was that while censorship did exist in Iraq, my minders were willing to listen patiently to my arguments for greater coverage opportunities, eager as they were to make the greatest use of the information opportunities of the global village. I, and the other journalists who came to join me in Baghdad, had some latitude to travel. I could discuss what I saw in long, live conversations with CNN's anchors. And amongst my most enthusiastic viewers were Pentagon intelligence and planning officers, and coalition bomber pilots in the Gulf, who were all eager to learn my latest bomb damage assessments and weather reports.

In Haiti's 1994 convulsive confrontation between the military junta and the Clinton administration, the American media in Port-au-Prince found itself on the side of the Washington officials anxious to dethrone the generals and return President Aristide to office. I found myself uncharacteristically basking in administration approval for justifiably highlighting the junta's miserable human rights record and blatant corruption.

Matters got out of hand one summer morning when, during a noisy demonstration outside the gates of the U.S. embassy, a mob of junta supporters attacked me and my crew with fists and boots.

Buried in falling bodies, I glanced up at the embassy roof and there, watching with seemingly indifferent interest, were the American ambassador, several aides and a score or so of armed Marines. Later, when I confronted embassy spokesman Stan Schrager he explained his inaction by pointing out, with gallows humor, that Washington was seeking valid reasons to invade Haiti and throw the generals out of office, "and your death at their hands would have been the perfect provocation to bring in the 101st Airborne Division." Thanks, Stan.

More often, however—in a world of global media—reporters with connections to international news organizations are of value to all sides in a conflict. Gunmen may target local journalists with impunity, but international correspondents are likely to be spared in recognition of their value as communicators.

Even remote, violent Chechnya is hip to the opportunities of the information age. During this past summer we bypassed Russian checkpoints and made our way to a remote village in the southern Caucasus Mountains where we interviewed the younger brother of fabled Chechen guerrilla fighter Shamil Basayev.

At the time the Russians were writing off the guerrillas as a spent force, but at this hideaway morale was high. Basayev's brother scoffed at reports of guerrilla weakness, but I pressed him, arguing that not one government in the whole world was offering the Chechens any support. "You're wrong," he laughed. "We have the support of the government of the international media, and you are one of its ambassadors."

The Government of the International Media—the worst fears come true of all those who in my lifetime have tried to censor, intimidate and lie to the press. It does have a great ring to it.

Peter Arnett, an international correspondent for CNN, has been covering the world's trouble spots since the late 1950s.

4

The Journey Is the Destination

Kathy Eldon

On July 12, 1993, my son, Dan Eldon, a Reuters photographer, was stoned to death by an angry mob in Mogadishu, Somalia. Dan and three colleagues, Hos Maina and Anthony Macharia of Reuters and Hansi Krauss of the Associated Press, had been summoned to the site of a brutal United Nations bombing that had left scores of people dead and dying. Enraged survivors turned on the journalists, murdering all four. Dan was 22 years old.

I was utterly devastated. Not only had I lost my only son, but I knew I was to blame for his death. After all, I had encouraged him to be a photographer. I had often taken him along to cover stories for *The Nation* newspaper in Kenya, where I worked for 10 years as a free-lance journalist. Dan was a familiar sight in the newsroom and from an early age contributed pictures to accompany my articles. I saw that Dan had a "photographer's eye" and badgered a visiting *National Geographic* photographer to sell me one of his old cameras to give to Dan as a Christmas present. A few years later, I bought used darkroom equipment so Dan could develop his own pictures. And always, I urged him to capture powerful images that told a story—and to use them to communicate important issues to as large an audience as possible.

It was certainly me, as an idealistic relic of the '60s, who encouraged Dan to believe he could "make a difference" and taught him from an early age to care about those less fortunate than he. When he was 12, he organized bake sales and sold T-shirts to raise money for an open-heart operation for a Kenyan child. Throughout high school, he supported a Masai woman and her family by selling her jewelry to visiting tourists. Dan even created a nightclub in our back garden and threw noisy parties for various charities. At 17, he scraped together enough money to buy an ancient Land Rover, which he named Deziree, and spent his weekends leading groups of timorous expatriate kids into the African bush to meet "real" Kenyans.

I encouraged Dan to be intrepid, sometimes even when it may have been dangerous. My husband never forgave me for telling the children how I drove to Nation House, the offices of *The Nation* newspaper, the day after the abortive coup of 1982 in Nairobi, when I narrowly missed being shot by a lone sniper holed up in the Hilton Hotel. But I had to go. One of my best friends, an Asian journalist, had disappeared when a mob swept through his house. I needed to help find him. Mike thought it a foolish act for the mother of two young children.

There was another reason why I knew I was responsible for Dan's death. When Dan was a senior in high school, Olympic Airlines sent me to Greece to write about the ancient ruins of Delphi. I found the visit deeply disturbing, for it was there that I first heard the message of the Oracle to "know thyself." I returned to Kenya to tell Dan what I had learned, adding the Shakespearean phrase, "and to thine own self be true." I urged him to seek his own truth and to follow it, no matter what.

Shortly afterwards, I heeded the words of the Oracle and realized that I had to leave my husband behind in Africa forever as I embarked on a long and painful journey of the soul. Though deeply saddened by my departure, Dan supported my decision and did not make me feel guilty. I only understood how hard it was for him after his death when I discovered a journal he had created during that period that reflected the intense anxieties of an 18-year-old grappling with the disintegration of his beloved family.

When I left home, Dan abandoned plans to attend a good college "in the east," and instead took a year off (he called it a "year on") to work at *Mademoiselle* magazine in New York. Newly transplanted from Nairobi, he found the city cold and unfriendly. He left three months later to drive an old brown Buick across America to enroll in a community college in Pasadena, Calif.

Homesick and yearning for Kenya, he founded a charity called Student Transport Aid, raised $17,000 and headed back to Africa, accompanied by 15 young people from seven different countries. In Nairobi, the students bought a Land Cruiser to supplement Deziree and drove across five countries to their destination, a refugee camp in Malawi. There, they donated the Land Cruiser to the Save the Children Fund and gave the rest of their money to build two wells for the refugees.

Every young person on that safari was transformed, no one more than Dan. He had discovered how a dream could be turned into reality—a reality that could help people help themselves. He returned to UCLA, this time eager to learn. He studied Japanese, philosophy, English literature and photography, voraciously devouring books on history and economics. He spent every spare hour working on his journals.

In the spring of 1992, Dan left three volumes of journals in a friend's garage in Los Angeles and returned to Nairobi for the summer. Although excited about being back in Kenya, he was looking forward to returning to UCLA, where, in the autumn, he planned to take courses in film, which he saw as his future career.

But it was during that summer that Dan heard rumors about a famine in Baidoa, a town in southern Somalia. Together with a young journalist from the *Philadelphia Inquirer,* he headed north in Deziree to see if the stories were true. What he saw in Baidoa sickened him. Yet somehow Dan, who as a boy couldn't even bear the sight of a cut finger, managed to photograph haunting images that captured the reality of the famine racing across Somalia. Through Reuters, his photos found their way into newspapers around the world and were among the first to trigger the world's response to the tragedy.

Dan, though horrified by what he had seen, returned again and again to Somalia. Eventually Reuters hired him as one of their youngest stringers. He quickly attached himself to older, more experienced photographers. Dan, a streetwise old Africa hand, worked Mogadishu like a pro, befriending beggars, diplomats and marines while running a thriving T-shirt and postcard business on the side.

In November of 1992, Dan visited me in London after a particularly harrowing stint in Somalia. Things weren't going well. The violence was escalating and his nerves were clearly on edge. Chain-smoking and irritable, he was battling with his feelings about his job—and women. He had recently been abandoned by a girlfriend, which had brought up long-repressed memories for him of my departure four years before. Our conversation was tortured. I was worried about his safety and hoped he might return to UCLA to finish his final year at college.

Dan was torn. He was excited about the prospect of studying film in California, but he felt his work in Africa was important. He showed me pictures he had taken for a book he was planning on Somalia. I could barely look at the shots of starving children, the pitiful images of wasted men and women, and a particularly haunting photo of an arrogant young soldier, cigarette butt hanging from his lips, standing in the midst of a ruined cathedral. I read what he had written:

> After my first trip to Somalia, the terror of being surrounded by violence and the horrors of the famine threw me into a dark depression. Even journalists who had covered many conflicts were moved to tears. But this was my first experience with war. Before Somalia I had only seen two dead bodies in my life. I have now seen hundreds, tossed into ditches like sacks. The worst things I could not photograph.
>
> One Sunday morning they brought in a pretty girl, wrapped in a colorful cloth. I saw that both her hands and feet had been severed by shrapnel. Someone had tossed a grenade in the market. She looked serene, like she was dead...but the nurse said that she would survive.
>
> It made me think of the whole country, Somalia will survive, but what kind of life is it for a people that have been so wounded? I don't know how these experiences have changed me, but I feel different.

Dan was different. In fact, I didn't know how to deal with the angry young man seated in front of me. We parted uneasily, our issues unresolved. For the next few months our communication was patchy and difficult, and I followed his movements from America by spotting his photographs in *Time, Newsweek, Der Stern* and on the front pages of the *New York Times, Herald Tribune* and *USA TODAY*.

Dan finally called me on my birthday, June 26, 1993. He was in Nairobi on a brief rest and sounded deeply fatigued and discouraged. He asked me why the world wasn't doing anything about the deteriorating situation in Somalia. As we talked, Dan began to explain how worried he was about how the horrific photographs he was taking might affect his mind. Slowly, he peeled back his tough journalist's exterior and allowed me inside. For the first time in months, our conversation flowed freely, and I realized there had been a profound change in my son. He had become a man. I was proud of him, proud of what he had achieved, but even more proud of who he had become.

Still, I was his mother, and I was worried. "Don't you think you've been there long enough?" I asked anxiously. "Isn't it time you came home?"

"Don't say that, Mum," he said. "I have to stay. My job isn't finished."

I suddenly remembered how Dan had supported me on the most difficult decision I had ever made. "OK," I answered. "No matter what, I'm proud of you. You're leading the life of your choice and I'm proud of you." I hung up quickly. A few minutes later the phone rang again.

"I love you." Dan said. "But we really need to talk. I'll send you a ticket to Nairobi."

The ticket never came.

Two weeks later Dan was dead, and I was left with horrible questions that tore at my soul. What if I hadn't left home? What if I had forced Dan to finish college? What if I hadn't taught my son to care about others? Maybe he would have graduated and done something sensible, something safe. After all, Dan could have been anything he wanted to be—an artist, a diplomat, an economist or a filmmaker. What if I hadn't encouraged Dan to be true to himself, no matter what? Would I be contemplating the possibility of playing with my grandchildren instead of cradling his journals in my arms? The questions haunted my dreams.

It has taken three years, but now I can finally sleep again, for I believe we both did what we had to do. Me, by teaching Dan the message of Delphi, and he, by following his heart no matter what.

Mohamed Amin, the Africa bureau chief for Reuters, wrote of Dan:

> It was his eye and brain and hand that captured forever the anguish of a nation. His pictures of Somalia are what millions who were not there carry around in their minds. His pictures stood out among the best—highlighting the agony of Somalia, as if asking the world to help. They appeared on the front pages of the world's top newspapers and magazines. At the age of 22, when most people his age were still wondering what they wanted to do, he had become a legend.
>
> Dan was an inspiration to young photographers. He was bright and funny, brave and handsome. He was a bright light which shone for a very short time. The light may no longer burn, but his work and memories will mean the flame is never extinguished.

I know Dan's death didn't make a shred of difference to the future of Somalia. But I don't believe that means Dan's life was in vain. He cared passionately about Africa and thought that by showing others what was wrong there, someone somewhere might just make it right. Dan saw the best in people and encouraged those he met to be the best they could possibly be. Although he lived for only 22 years, those years were filled with a sense of excitement and meaning that few people realize in a full lifetime.

Dan sought to live with "energy, sincerity, clarity of vision, creativity." His mission: "Safari as a way of life. To explore the unknown and known, distant and near, and to record in detail, with the eyes of a child, any beauty (of the flesh or otherwise), humor, irony, traces of utopia or hell. Select your team with care, but when in doubt, take on new crew and give them a chance."

Kathy Eldon, formerly a free-lance journalist for The Nation *newspaper in Nairobi, Kenya, and media consultant in England, now runs Creative Visions, a film production company.*

5

Press Freedom—Balkan Style

Kati Marton

The guns that felled 45 reporters covering the war in Bosnia are quiet now. But media in the former Yugoslavia are just as effectively controlled by their authoritarian governments' use of more subtle measures.

After a 10-day fact-finding trip to Sarajevo, Belgrade and Zagreb, I am convinced a healthy democratic opposition will not take root here without much stronger Western pressure on Serbian, Croatian and Bosnian leaders. In all three capitals, I conducted dozens of interviews with local journalists and the three leaders who prevent them from doing their jobs "without fear or favor"—Slobodan Milosevic, Franjo Tudjman and Alija Izetbegovic. All three promised to uphold the right to free speech and free press in Dayton, Ohio, and all three are falling far short of delivering on that promise. Yet Milosevic, Tudjman and Izetbegovic, lacking clear mandates from their own populations, are vulnerable to outside pressure.

The Balkan media's plight is urgent. It was the media in Belgrade, Zagreb and, to a much lesser degree, Sarajevo that stoked the ethnic passions unleashing the war. It is now essential for the security of Europe and ultimately the United States that we aid in restoring a free media in Serbia, Croatia and Bosnia.

The situation is critical in Bosnia. Without a free press, the dream of reviving a multiethnic society after years of savage violence will remain just that.

Sarajevo is remarkably serene now. Cafes sprout seemingly overnight on war-battered squares. But it is still too dangerous for Bosnian journalists to cover more than a thin sliver of the country the peace accords led them to believe was theirs. During my visit to the heroic Sarajevo daily, *Oslobodjenje,* editor Emir Habul stood in front of a large map in his dingy office and pointed out how far his reporters dare go for news: Sarajevo, Ilidza, Vogosca, Visoko, up to Zenica and Tuzla and the Bihac pocket. In short, they can cover no more than 20 percent of the country. They dare not penetrate the Serb-held areas of Banja Luka, Brcko, Pale Zepa or Gorazde, or the Croat-controlled western part of Mostar. The bold ones who venture farther come back shaken from the experience. They return with stories of how Serb militia loyal to Radovan Karadzic, the indicted president of the Bosnian Serbs, spotted their Sarajevo plates, pulled them off the road and hauled them in for "questioning."

Every conversation in Sarajevo circles back to Karadzic. It was he who sent precise instructions to Serbs in the Sarajevo suburbs of Illitca and Grabovitze to burn their apartments as they evacuated them for the returning Moslems. "Turn on the gas," they were told. "Open the oven door. Light a candle. Shut the windows. Open the front door. Leave quickly. A fine explosion will soon follow. Do it or we'll do it for you."

So it is all the people of Sarajevo, not only reporters, who fear the continued power of Karadzic. As they replace the plastic sheets that cover their blown-out windows with real glass and sweep the mountains of rubble from their front stoops, they keep one watchful eye toward Pale, his stronghold. They cannot trust the future while Karadzic is free.

And not all the infringements on a free press come from Karadzic. In Bosnia, like elsewhere, most people get their news from television. Yet only one of nine transmitters survived the war. What limited television there is, is under the control of President Alija Izetbegovic's ruling party and thus rarely criticizes his government. Opposition candidates like former Prime Minister Haris Silajdic, who at least during the election was a strong voice for independent media, find it hard to get their message out.

Ironically, Radio Free Europe, deemed a relic of the Cold War elsewhere and never before heard in Yugoslavia, has become the most popular radio in Bosnia. Until the Bosnians' own media system is firmly in place, most people think RFE's broadcasts are as close as they'll get to the straight story.

Ten miles east of Sarajevo, from the shabby former ski resort of Pale, the capitol of the self-styled Republic of Srpska, Karadzic keeps fanning the flames of hate. Pale TV, the only Bosnian Serb television available throughout Bosnia, reinforces the Serbs' siege mentality via its nightly news, portraying Muslims, Croats and most of the outside world as hostile toward Serbs and their indicted war criminal leader. "By taking away our leaders," Pale TV once announced, "they wish to control us."

As an antidote to this poisonous flow of disinformation, the Vienna-based Organization for Security and Cooperation, charged with preparing the ground for the upcoming elections, is raising funds to set up an independent television network. Equal time for all candidates will be its mandate. But Open Broadcast News, as the new network will be called, faces a Sisyphian task. It must counter years of strident nationalistic propaganda and indoctrination with the tempered message of mutual tolerance.

In Belgrade and Zagreb, independent media are controlled by the use of "financial police," government "accountants" who swoop down on opposition press and usually find their bookkeeping wanting. On April 25, such accountants swept into the office of the Croatian weekly *Panorama,* which challenged the Tudjman party line, and ordered all staff to leave within 15 minutes. The magazine still remains shut down. The reason: alleged "failure to meet technical, health and ecological standards necessary for operating."

When I asked President Tudjman why his government was suing another independent paper, *Novi List,* for a ruinous sum, his mask of benevolence slipped. Tudjman erupted from his arm chair in my direction. "Madame!" he exploded, and I commanded myself not to blink. He ordered an aide to fetch a pile of newspapers. "There!" he pointed at the cover of the satirical weekly, *Feral Tribune,* which featured Tudjman's face atop Rambo's body. "Would any other world leader put up with this?" he asked. "All the democratically elected ones," I replied. "President Clinton also gets press he doesn't like," I told him. "I think it comes with being a public servant."

Another technique used by both Milosevic and Tudjman to quiet the irritating voices of dissent is using privatization laws, which claim that formerly state-controlled media were "improperly privatized." Serbian police entered Belgrade's Studio B and pulled the plug using that device. Now all Serb TV is under President Milosevic's control. But Milosevic assured me (revealing his ignorance of the ways of the free press) that he instructed the media to tamp down its former anti-Moslem and anti-Croat fervor, and get behind the Dayton Accords.

Milosevic, who keeps an iron grip on all state-controlled enterprises, including the newsprint industry, manipulates the independent dailies' circulation. *Nasa Borba,* the major independent daily in Serbia, struggles to reach its more than 10,000 readers. But *Politika,* the pro-Milosevic paper, never suffers from a newsprint shortage and reaches 300,000 readers. To go from *Nasa Borba*'s shabby offices to *Politika*'s high-tech home bristling with security men is to understand the effective uses of press control in Serbia. *Politika*'s editor, Hadzi Antic, a well-known Belgrade operator, described his editorial policy as "inclined toward the official story." He spoke into a cellular phone wittily brand-named "Mobtel," which I saw advertised in a magazine, for 16 thousand deutsche marks. Antic, a beefy man who wears his hair pulled into a tiny ponytail, said that if other papers have circulation problems it's because they're no good.

Antic publishes in a city, Belgrade, that feels dejected, apathetic and sour. The tentative steps toward democratization that preceded this tragic war have been supplanted by a new reality where reformers are squeezed into a small ghetto while sly dealers prosper. In a region with no tradition of a free and responsible media, raucous voices are to be expected. Yet it is precisely the profusion of these voices that will give people reason to believe that arguments can be settled in print and on the airwaves and not on the battlefield.

The picture is not without hope. Here, as elsewhere in the region, the voices of fiery nationalism are quiet. These leaders are not the implacable dictators of the past. They are "soft" autocrats, vulnerable to pressure. When I reminded Milosevic of his earlier promise to reregister the Soros Open Society Fund, which he had once again banned (and which has virtually kept independent media alive in Serbia) he sighed and said, "[Foreign Minister] Milotunovic will take care of it." After weeks of stalling, Milosevic finally gave the go-ahead to reopen the Fund.

There are many pressure points. Serbia badly wants still-remaining sanctions lifted. Bosnia, the only real victim in the war, as well as Serbia and Croatia need Western investment, IMF loans, European Union membership, respectability. A price must be exacted for all those things, and part of that price should be the one ingredient that separates a democracy from every other form of government: a free press. That is the only durable way to check the demagogues' next urge toward the quick fix of hate.

Kati Marton, an author and a 1987–88 Media Studies Center fellow, is a member of the board of directors of the Committee to Protect Journalists. Her books include The Polk Conspiracy *(1990). Her essay is based on a fact-finding mission to the former Yugoslavia in April and May of 1996. She is married to Richard C. Holbrooke, former U.S. assistant secretary of state and main architect of the Bosnian peace plan.*

Part III

Government Repression

6

Grim Prospects for Hong Kong

John Schidlovsky

Hong Kong's imminent return to China as of July 1, 1997, is one of the great historical events of the late 20th century. At one stroke, it will virtually end the European colonial era (Portugal's colony of Macau reverts to China in 1999), while at the same time posing this dramatic question: What happens when one of the world's most freewheeling and least regulated societies is taken over by one of the most control-minded regimes on earth?

For some years now, most signs have pointed to Hong Kong's economic vitality surviving, perhaps even increasing, under China's promise to allow "one country, two systems" for the next 50 years. After all, China is already the largest single investor in Hong Kong and has much to lose by precipitating change. Beijing has long since demonstrated its own faith in the kind of unbridled capitalism that has made Hong Kong a global financial center.

But in China, as in some other parts of Asia, dynamic economies are one thing; free speech, free expression and free press are quite another. China is merely the largest country in Asia to produce high economic growth year after year while muzzling political and intellectual freedoms. The model has worked in Singapore, Malaysia and Indonesia. It used to work just fine in Taiwan and South Korea, where authoritarian leaders nurtured impressive economic growth until middle-class-based democratic movements resulted in less repressive governments.

In the long run, China and Hong Kong may experience a similar process of democratization that would result in easing of press curbs. But for the moment, prospects for press freedom in Hong Kong are grim. Local journalists are increasingly convinced that China will not tolerate the kind of independent and aggressive reporting that has characterized the colony's media under recent British colonial rule. (To be sure, during the height of China's Cultural Revolution in the late 1960s, British authorities in Hong Kong were not always as tolerant of free speech as they are today. Young Hong Kong activists such as Tsang Tak-sing—now the editor of the pro-China daily *Ta Kung Pao*—were imprisoned for their anti-colonial agitation.)

In recent months, statements by Chinese officials on the media's role after July 1 have added to Hong Kong journalists' apprehensions. "With just one year to go to the end of British colonial rule in Hong Kong, there have been alarming developments which undoubtedly jeopardize the right to freedom of expression," said a report issued June 30 this year by the Hong Kong Journalists Association (HKJA), an industry-wide journalists' union with about 650 members that has been an active force for several years in protesting threats to press freedom. The new report, the latest in an annual series issued by the HKJA, was entitled "China's Challenge," significantly shifts the responsibility for press freedom issues squarely on Beijing and away from the British colonial administration.

Journalists in Hong Kong have been particularly alarmed by comments made by Lu Ping, director of China's Hong Kong and Macau Affairs Office, in a series of interviews and press conferences in May and June. While assuring Hong Kong "there will certainly be freedom of press after 1997," Lu went on to say that the media would "absolutely not" be allowed to "advocate" controversial political views such as favoring the independence of Hong Kong or Taiwan, which China regards as part of its own territory.

"That wouldn't be allowed. Certainly wouldn't be allowed," Lu said. "There are certain national laws [by] which Hong Kong should also abide." The HKJA called Lu's remarks "highly threatening and dangerous to freedom of expression." Under current Hong Kong law, residents are quite free to advocate political views as part of their rights to free speech that the current British governor, Chris Patten, said "should be guaranteed" without any exceptions after July 1.

Under an agreement signed between Britain and China in 1984, Hong Kong, a British colony since 1841, will become a "Special Administrative Region" of China. Most worrisome to Hong Kong's journalists is Article 23 in the Basic Law—the mini-constitution that will serve Hong Kong for the first 50 years of Chinese rule—that allows China to take any action it wants against "treason, secession, sedition, subversion against the Central People's Government, or theft of state secrets." If

Chinese authorities decide that a newspaper or a journalist's reports
fall into any of these categories, they can prosecute him despite all
pledges of press freedom.

Still fresh in the minds of many Hong Kong journalists is the case of
Xi Yang, a reporter for the Hong Kong newspaper *Ming Pao,* who was
sentenced in 1994 to 12 years in jail in China for "stealing state secrets" for his reporting of undisclosed bank interest rates. Ivan Tong,
past chairman of the HKJA, has said Xi's health is reportedly failing in
jail and has asked Beijing for his release on medical grounds.

Beijing officials other than Lu Ping have also repeatedly reminded
Hong Kong journalists of the need to be "patriotic," which Hong Kong
journalists see as a clear message for them to subordinate their journalistic principles to Beijing's political priorities. Late last year, Zhang
Junsheng told journalists that "to love our mother country is a noble
sentiment." Zhang is none other than deputy director of the Hong Kong
branch of Xinhua, the official Chinese news agency that also acts as
Beijing's diplomatic and political arm in Hong Kong.

What makes the coming collision of Hong Kong and Chinese phi-
losophies on the press unavoidable is the fact that China's leaders have
operated for nearly 50 years on the assumption that the media must be
"patriotic" by serving the interests of the state and the Communist Party.
Independent reporting is simply not in the party lexicon.

As if to remind journalists of their traditional role, early this year
Xinhua published a mammoth new *Dictionary of Chinese Journalism,*
an encyclopedic compendium of what Xinhua itself called "a reference
book essential to journalists." With 4,991 entries and more than 2.3
million words, the volume attempts to give a history of journalism in
modern China along with a reminder of its role as a propagandist for
the Party.

"The chapter about theory, which is extremely important," said
Xinhua's own story on the book, "highlights the guidelines of Chinese
journalism based on Marxism-Leninism, Mao Zedong Thought and
Deng Xiaoping's theories about socialism with Chinese characteristics. The dictionary, which is very orthodox ideologically, emphasizes
the class nature of the Communist press, its proletarian principles, and
its mission as a mouthpiece."

To be sure, the Chinese media have been ignoring ideological principles for years and have, in fact, been encouraged by the government
to act more independently—at least in commercial matters. (It is precisely because Chinese journalists have been ignoring Marxism-

Leninism that such an "orthodox" dictionary was likely produced by increasingly isolated hard-liners.) As China's free-market reforms have spread, the old official media have been weaned of their traditional subsidies and have been ordered to sink or swim in the marketplace. Government subsidies to Xinhua, for example, have been decreasing by about 7 percent a year. Forced to acquire readers and advertising, the media has plunged headlong into entertainment and sensationalism, a phenomenon that author and China specialist Orville Schell described in the summer 1995 issue of this journal in "Maoism vs. Media in the Marketplace."

Despite the plethora of glossy new publications, talk-radio programs and slick television shows available to Chinese consumers, serious journalistic efforts remain tightly monitored and controlled by the government. Editors at all Chinese newspapers must pass on to officials of the party's Propaganda Department any remotely controversial stories. Journalists who have a reputation for activism or who specialize in investigative reporting are given few opportunities to cover meaningful subjects. An example of a talented journalist who is, in effect, professionally shelved, is Dai Qing, a dynamic writer who specialized in environmental and investigative reporting. After the 1989 Tiananmen demonstrations she was imprisoned, as were other activist journalists, before being allowed to leave the country. Having returned to China, she is forbidden to write for mass-circulation publications.

While carefully monitoring what Chinese journalists produce, the government has been less successful in keeping out information from the outside world. Despite a ban on satellite dishes that receive foreign television transmissions, these dishes have proliferated up and down the coast of China, where economic development has been centered. Another growing source of information for the public is the Internet. Although Chinese Minister of Posts and Telecommunications Wu Jichuan said last year that Beijing would "increase its control over information" available through this global computer network, in fact, access to the Internet has increased dramatically. Like Singapore and other nations that are wary of "subversive" information on the Internet, China hasn't quite figured out how to censor the system.

However, when it comes to more traditional sources of outside information, Xinhua has not hesitated to assert its control. Earlier this year, it announced it would take over distribution (and charge a fee for doing so) of all financial news and information provided within China by foreign news agencies, such as Reuters, Dow Jones, Bloomberg and others. Xinhua already controls the distribution of foreign news reports within China.

The Xinhua announcement provoked strong criticism by foreign companies, who fear they'll lose their competitive edge in providing real-time financial news to companies, both foreign and Chinese, doing business in China. Protests by domestic and overseas firms, especially if applied during future business negotiations with Beijing authorities, may, in the long run, compel Chinese officials to loosen their grip over news and financial information. Meanwhile, in June, Xinhua announced plans to set up its own financial news and information service, which would compete with the foreign providers whose services Xinhua will now be distributing. Foreign news agency officials are skeptical that Xinhua will be fair-minded or expeditious in distributing competitors' news.

In Hong Kong, foreign news agencies are warily watching Xinhua's tactics in China, wondering if similar strategies are planned for Hong Kong. So far, Chinese authorities have said little about how foreign correspondents and global media companies based in Hong Kong will operate. Beijing currently requires all China-based foreign correspondents to register with the Foreign Ministry and limits their travel rights, and it is believed likely that China may do the same with Hong Kong-based foreign correspondents some time after the transition.

As for Hong Kong journalists, many of them are getting ready to accommodate themselves to the new regime. A group of pro-China newspapers has formed the Hong Kong Federation of Journalists as an alternative to the HKJA. This new organization, made up of papers either funded directly by China or heavily supported with advertisements from mainland companies, has begun trying to reassure those in the media that nothing at all will change next year—provided the press acts "responsibly."

"We as journalists hope we will enjoy more and more press freedom," Edmund Chan Kin-ming, the chairman of the new federation, wrote in a recent op-ed article in one Hong Kong daily. "On the other hand, we cannot forget that we are governed by existing laws stating that we cannot libel someone or report false news."

Will the Hong Kong people be allowed to hold the annual memorial demonstrations on June 4 to commemorate those killed in 1989 by Chinese troops in Beijing? Will the press be allowed to give prominent coverage to these demonstrations? Addressing that subject, Chan's reply contained some ominous undertones: "As long as they are approved by the government, events like the peaceful June 4 gathering in Victoria Park will continue. And, of course, the media will be allowed to cover them. Right now, they are peaceful. Next year, the nature of these types of gatherings may change. Let's wait and see."

One of the main concerns of the HKJA has been trying to convince the British colonial government to repeal a series of what the HKJA terms "draconian" laws that journalists fear could be used by China to shut down publications or to arrest individual journalists on the pretext of public security. Long-standing laws such as the Official Secrets Act, or the Emergency Regulations Ordinance, while rarely if ever invoked against the press by British authorities in the past, give the government potentially widespread powers of censorship.

Unless these laws are amended, post-1997 authorities could use them to repress dissenters. Such laws are doubly disturbing because, as the HKJA annual report says, "as powers inherited from the British colonial administration, their use may be easier to justify and defend."

Another concern for Hong Kong journalists, particularly those in broadcasting, is what will happen to the local broadcast authority, Radio and Television Hong Kong (RTHK). Though government owned and subsidized, RTHK retains editorial independence along the lines of the British Broadcasting Corp. and produces a variety of news programs for Hong Kong's commercial stations. However, Beijing has indicated that it may try to use RTHK as a mouthpiece for its official news, since that is how it defines the role of its own government-run broadcasters. RTHK officials say they will resist efforts to change the authority's independent perspective, though they may be legally powerless in preventing China from controlling what ultimately gets on the air.

Other Hong Kong broadcasters, too, are uncertain of how much journalistic freedom they will be allowed to exercise after July 1. The two main commercial stations, ATV (Asia Television Ltd.) and TVB (Television Broadcasts Ltd.), have bowed repeatedly to Beijing in the past two years by refusing to air sensitive documentaries about China and dropping a popular current affairs talk show, "News Tease," that often featured criticism of Beijing authorities. Meanwhile, the privately run Cable TV firm has incurred China's displeasure by presenting the BBC World Service, which is banned on the mainland. The World Service is an old irritant to the Chinese government; after Chinese complaints about BBC broadcasts, Rupert Murdoch voluntarily removed it from his Star TV offerings.

Clearly, as of July 1, 1997, it will take Herculean efforts to preserve, much less expand, Hong Kong's press freedom. Optimists believe that a combination of strong-willed journalists, continued public pressure from both domestic and international watchdog groups and China's own recognition of the importance of the free flow of information will succeed in maintaining an open and independent press. But given the signals that Beijing has been sending for the past several years now, it would be naive and unrealistic to expect anything other than a contraction of press freedom, along with reductions of academic, religious, artistic and social freedoms. Until China's prevailing attitudes change, Hong Kong will have to look well beyond 1997 to see a day when it can again experience the freedoms it now enjoys.

John Schidlovsky, a former Asia-based correspondent with the Baltimore Sun, *was director of The Freedom Forum Asian Center in Hong Kong.*

7

Self-Censorship in Hong Kong

Orville Schell

Reporters for Hong Kong's free, open and diverse press are coming to understand that pieces that may appear "unfriendly" to Beijing affect both their parent company's chances of getting into China's rapidly expanding media markets as well as their immediate employer's ability to survive in Hong Kong after China assumes power on July 1, 1997. Many reporters quite honestly confess that they feel caught in a growing tendency toward self-censorship. In a meeting at The Freedom Forum Asian Center, members of the Hong Kong press corps offered these views.

Courage of Hong Kong Reporters

What worries us is not whether reporters themselves will be courageous, but whether their news organizations—which are now all looking for market share in China itself—will support us when we are courageous. Most news organizations here are looking to get into business in China and have thus allowed a climate of self-censorship to creep in. So what gets covered is not so much a question of our willingness as reporters to be courageous and to sacrifice.

—Ivan Tong, deputy editor in chief for finance, Ming Pao

Sacrifices of Press Freedom in Hong Kong

I don't think we've sacrificed anything yet, but the psychologically chilling effect of cases such as Xi Yang's are obvious on those of us who cover China. We are reluctant to send reporters to China for fear of having another Xi Yang arrest on our hands. [*Ming Pao* reporter Xi

Yang was arrested in 1994 for allegedly revealing state secrets and was subsequently sentenced to 12 years by a Chinese court.] And when we are blacklisted so that it is hard to get in to cover China, that, too, is a very effective chilling tool for journalists. All of these things have a very practical impact on our news gathering.

—Daisy Li, reporter, Ming Pao

Outlook under Chinese Government

They deny that we should be really independent. They just don't believe in it because of their tradition of mass thought. For them, journalists are just servants of the government. Moreover, they think that if they can grab hold of Hong Kong's media outlets, it will make the situation more secure for them.

—Mak Yin Ting, reporter, Radio Television Hong Kong

The Future

There are two options for us. We can cooperate or confront, and you can see quite clearly the different postures different people and groups have adopted.... We are in a very delicate situation. China is under a kind of siege mentality and is taking an increasingly tough line against Hong Kong. Generally speaking I think that we still need to apply pressure on China, although I'm not really sure if pressure will work.

—Terry Cheng, editor, Hong Kong Standard

If Hong Kong speaks in just one voice, it will be very dangerous.

—Daisy Li

Orville Schell, a 1995–96 Media Studies Center fellow, is dean of the Graduate School of Journalism and research associate at the Center for Chinese Studies at the University of California, Berkeley.

8

Russian Reporters—
Between a Hammer and an Anvil

Iosif M. Dzyaloshinsky

In 1995, the Forestry Committee of Leningrad *Oblast*—a region of Russia—sued a number of newspapers in defense of its reputation. According to the Committee, the newspapers *Nevskoe vremya, Segodnya, Vecherny Peterburg, Reklama-Shans* and *Smena* damaged the reputation of the Committee and its chairman, Andrei Gosudarev, by publishing the Russian Green Party's charges that the transfer of protected state land to small farming plots was illegal.

As became clear during the hearings, the Committee did not dispute any of the facts. It only demanded that in the future any publications about the state of forestry management in Leningrad *Oblast* be checked ahead of time with Mr. Gosudarev.

The events in Leningrad *Oblast* are an extreme yet illuminating example of the challenges that journalists face in Russia when they confront government authorities accustomed to the compliant media of the communist era. Worse, such holdovers from the mind-set of the old regime are not the only challenges to independent and uncoerced reporting in Russia.

Ten years of *perestroika,* radical market reforms, democracy and the breakup of the Soviet Union have given Russia freedom of speech and the independent media to guarantee it. Yet the condition of the mass media in Russia is still shaky, and sometimes the price of independence is fatally high. The mass media and journalists are caught between the market, with its economic pressures, and the authorities, who try to control them by withholding information, issuing economic threats and pressuring journalists.

Nevertheless, while the situation of the Russian media is fairly typical of post-Soviet states, Russian journalists are more prepared for survival in market conditions and struggles with authorities than their colleagues in other republics because Russia has advanced further on the path of economic and political reform, and consequently its journalists are better prepared to meet the challenges of the post-Soviet order.

In early 1996, new Russian laws on state support for the media came into force and signaled the larger transformation of a press created to serve the needs of a totalitarian society into a press striving to become an integral part of a market economy and a democratic state.

First, the structure of the mass media has changed. Before *perestroika* the most influential medium was the print press. Now, it is television. Rising newsprint prices make papers expensive, while television is free for the watching and television sets are cheap. The shift from two channels to as many as seven and improved programming have made television more attractive to viewers.

Overall, there is a tendency for more and more Russians to read local newspapers and watch national television. Print press merits special attention, however, because Russians tend to find it more credible than broadcasting and because it is their primary source of local news.

The financial situation of the mass media is less hopeful. All publications are required to register with the government, and 85 percent of all registered publications receive state or other subsidies that provide economic sustenance but compromise independence. In the 89 regions that comprise Russia—republics, *krais* and *oblasts*—almost all publications receive some form of subsidy from the state, local authorities or so-called sponsors. Among publications that circulate nationally, the situation is better: 40 percent claim complete financial independence.

The federal government has always subsidized national newspapers directly, but its role in subsidizing local newspapers was simply to mandate to the local governments which newspapers would be supported without providing any of the funding. In 1995, the federal government decentralized the subsidies, allocating to the local governments decision-making authority in granting subsidies. But at local levels of government, funds for the press are typically the lowest priority in budgets, providing for neither newer newspaper equipment and printing presses nor minimum salaries for journalists, whose profession is one of the lowest paid in Russia.

While the best-paid Russian journalists earn the equivalent of $5,000 a month, most earn $100 to $200 a month. (A secretary working for a commercial firm, as opposed to an agency in the poorly paid state sector, might earn as much as $350 per month.) Because of their unprofitability generally, newspapers are not in a financial position to pay their journalists even average wages.

With journalists' salaries and honoraria so much lower than the rates that commercial firms, political parties and other organizations pay for illegal information services, the level of corruption and payoffs among journalists and editors is inevitably rising.

In addition to the state and political parties, there is a third channel of support for the mass media: sponsorship by entrepreneurial, commercial and financial structures. It is no secret that large financial groups and individual banks seek to play a more active role in the press business.

There is nothing wrong with this, but society has a right to know who, and at what level, provides financial and material resources for whom, especially when talking about such a sensitive area as the media. There are currently no legal means or organizational mechanisms that would allow oversight of this process.

Along with all the economic problems of the press, journalists must also contend with the growing complexity of relations with the government. Authorities still try to legislate media activities, oversee observance of legislation and interfere constantly with the activities of journalists. Their means: the 1991 Law of the USSR on the Press and Other Mass Media, and the Law of the Russian Federation on Mass Media, which enshrined the concept of publications' "founders." A holdover from the days of communism, a founder—which can be a person, organization or local government—can appoint or fire an editor.

In late 1991 and early 1992 most founders who were heads of government structures preferred to show that they were liberals by founding mass media and not interfering in their activities. In 1995, however, founders—especially at the level of regional or local administration—contemplated the prospect of elections and concluded that media subordinated to their interests would help them at the polls. At the same time, the founders were caught up in a general trend throughout Russia towards strengthening the executive branch of government at all levels.

Throughout Russia, there have been attempts to prevent journalists from writing about certain topics or people. Freedom of information questions have acquired unexpected resonance. Flaws in Russian press law allow officials either to hide objective information or to dispense disinformation without breaking any existing rules. Information was, of course, hard to acquire earlier, but what has happened in the past few years, especially related to the war in Chechnya, has made the problem even more obvious.

Speaking at the Forum of the Democratic Press on Sept. 1, 1995, Russian President Boris Yeltsin said that many state agencies hide valuable information from journalists and demanded that official bodies become more open with information. The president did not say anything new to the journalists, but the fact that the head of state focused attention on the matter points out that this issue has, as they say, ripened.

Research conducted by the author in 1995 showed that about 70 percent of journalists working in the regional media have confronted situations in which authorities refuse to divulge information. Since then, the figure has risen to 80 percent. Journalists rate law enforcement the least responsive of government agencies. As a result, many journalists now consider it normal to buy information from officials and paid sources.

As the conflict intensifies between supporters of the old, authoritarian way of dealing with the media and advocates of new, more democratic forms of journalism, there has been a sharp rise in physical pressure on journalists in both outlying regions and big cities. Irina Chernova, a young journalist who was investigating police corruption in Volgograd, was beaten unconscious by police. In Tarusa, another journalist, Tatyana Fedyaeva, was carried out of a supposedly open government meeting by police officers.

And there are new threats: One can accidentally harm the interests of powerful financial or criminal organizations and within hours lose one's job with no hope of finding new work. Cases of direct physical violence, including murder, have become more common for journalists. Grenades explode in journalists' apartments. Square-shouldered young men with crew cuts appear in the offices of editors of provincial newspapers investigating certain dark stories and quietly suggest putting an end to the investigation. The police in Volgograd have organized, at great expense, round-the-clock protection for the journalist Chernova, who dared to inform the readers of *Komsomolskaya Pravda* about the connections of the several local law enforcement agencies with organized crime.

All this is painfully reminiscent of the foreign detective novels we read in our youth. Today, in Russia, they are a reality.

Journalists are poorly prepared to act against such attacks because the old unity of journalists has fallen apart. In its place there is the snobbery of Moscow journalists and the envious resentment of their regional counterparts. The media are further divided into those that receive state or other subsidies and those that do not. Journalists denied access to this feeding trough are irritated. And those who receive budget money do not hide their derisive attitude toward those who receive financing from private capital.

The difference between the Moscow media and regional media is obvious. The financial resources of the country are concentrated in Moscow, along with Russia's best intellectual forces, information sources and communications technology. But most importantly, authorities in the Kremlin and Moscow have always refrained from crude methods of managing the media.

Of course, Moscow media are not completely free from the influence of the authorities. Sometimes the heads of the Moscow media are invited, collectively or individually, to high offices. Representatives of the elite and heads of the media now meet at informal lunches and dinners, a relatively new phenomenon for Russia. These are seen as civilized, accepted methods of lobbying.

But Moscow journalists can resist attempts at pressure. Rank-and-file Moscow reporters, despite their complaints, are independent enough and always have the opportunity to move to another paper. And in the top ranks, Moscow editors have shown that they can not only argue with the authorities but also fight with them.

The situation in the regions is significantly worse: Typical Soviet methods of press management are still common. Editors are called in to see the governor or the president's representative and threatened with a funding cut, revocation of a lease or withdrawal of printing privileges. A typical example: Gov. Chub of the southern *oblast* of Rostov, angered by the appearance in a city paper of three simultaneous articles critical of President Yeltsin, ordered the immediate sacking of the editor in chief.

Journalists, weak and divided as a profession, are practically unable to defend themselves from the encroachments of local tsars. Reporters from independent regional newspapers and broadcasters are not accredited at major events and are not given official information.

Despite calls to preserve unity in the ranks of the Union of Journalists of Russia, there are more and more associations of professionals that keep formal ties to the Union but that are in reality sailing off in other directions. Since *perestroika,* the Union has lost the funding and government links that once made it helpful to journalists. Instead, reporters curry favor with government officials. This is not the best way to achieve independent journalism, but it does provide breathing room for reporters who have to deal with their immediate crises. Organizations like the Glasnost Defense Fund do important work to protect the rights and freedoms of journalists, but they are too few and too weak.

The mood of journalists is also affected by the fact that the mass media have lost their Soviet-era influence as "collective propagandist organizers." During the *perestroika* period, critical and politicized journalism brought success. But with the collapse of the democratic euphoria, journalists have lost their leading role and come into conflict with society.

Since the late 1980s, many Russians have lost their belief in notions of democracy and market economics that invigorated the *perestroika*-era press. For may people, the market means poverty and democracy means chaos.

In this situation, journalists are left with two choices. One is the easy but very dubious and almost masochistic path to success—to become purveyors of social disenchantment while maintaining a democratic image. The other choice is to rethink radically the journalist's role, and seek not to convince the people to vote for a particular candidate but to monitor the power structure to help the electorate make a free and informed choice.

Journalists found themselves in a particularly difficult situation during the recent presidential elections. Many foreign and some Russian journalists are very critical of the fact that many famous journalists, well-known for their adherence to the ideals of objective and unbiased journalism, announced their support for Yeltsin quite openly. Responding to such accusations, Igor Malashenko, president of NTV (Independent Television, the only national nongovernmental television network) said: "The dilemma is very simple: If we follow the rules by being strictly objective, professional, unbiased and nonpartisan and tomorrow Zyuganov [the Communist Party presidential candidate] wins, then we will know that we have dug our own grave with our own hands. If, to avoid this scenario, we stand on the side of Yeltsin and start to help him, this means that the mass media will have become mass propaganda. There are pitfalls everywhere."

Although the conception of the press as a player in political struggles has been widespread in journalistic circles, common sense has won out and the press has turned away from the great honor of considering itself to be part of the power structure. In this formula, journalists should accurately reflect reality and not concentrate on what happens in the swollen minds of some of our commentators.

But the legal status of journalists in Russia is still uncertain. While there is no First Amendment in Russia, there is a special law on the media (which recently celebrated its fifth anniversary) that fully conforms to accepted democratic standards. There are also, however, other mutually contradictory laws, most of which are designed to defend the authorities from being tried in the court of public opinion. The media are also governed by many presidential decrees and governmental regulations whose authors completely ignore previous laws and decrees. When the need for these temporary regulations ends, the authorities forget to invalidate them and leave them there to clutter the legislative landscape.

Of course, things could be worse. In other post-Soviet states the condition of the media is even more difficult. Russian journalists may criticize the president and the government for their indifference to the problems of media professionals, but they understand that such indifference is better than the great attention to press affairs shown in places like Belarus, where President Alexander Lukashenka has fired editors, and Turkmenistan, where government pressure induces journalists to conform to an official line.

What does the future hold? The most pessimistic scenario assumes that social conflict interrupts plans for the country's transition to a market economy and democracy. If this happens, Russia will be threatened with both internal and external catastrophes. A totalitarian system of control over the mass media will be restored and publications like *Pravda* will be preeminent.

The other scenario, which many specialists consider more probable, assumes that for the foreseeable future Russia will be a measured authoritarian state with a mixed state-capitalist economy. In this scenario, the state will at first try to control the mass media through economic and legal levers. There will be special state programs to support the press.

But there is simply not enough money in Russia to do this, and the prospect of journalists scrambling for limited government funds is unattractive. Ultimately, the government must create the conditions for the media to survive on their own and replace direct subsidies with tax breaks.

In 1996 new laws will be passed to regulate media relations with all elements of society. In all likelihood these measures will fail to bring the expected results. The state will then reject attempts at direct regulation of the mass media, which will allow the full development of market mechanisms for the media.

The press will then be forced to appeal for financial help not to the state but to commercial structures and directly to the readers. Newspapers and magazines will become normal commercial enterprises acting by the laws of the market.

The most mass-oriented and dynamically developing medium will continue to be television. As market reforms progress, many print media will close, forcing firings and cutbacks. Periodical publications that survive will become more businesslike and modern and will respond to the changing demands of the readers. The publications with the greatest chance for success are local, independent, general-interest, depoliticized, largely informational publications with a serious, businesslike tone.

Changes in professional work conditions will demand the resolution of several problems related to the legal regulation of the print media. Most of all this means that reliable and simple access to socially important information must be ensured for journalists, including those who are not accredited to specific newspapers or television or radio companies.

Great effort must also be applied to make sure that the legal concept of hindering the professional work of a journalist remains in the criminal code and is actually enforced.

The Russian press, as in other post-Soviet states, is moving fitfully toward the model of relations between government, society and media that are characteristic of countries with established market and democratic traditions. The faster the press can move along this path, the more confidently we can speak of the irreversibility of the transformations that will ensure both freedom of speech and independent journalism in Russia.

Iosif M. Dzyaloshinsky is chairman of the Standing Commission on Freedom of Information, a program of the Russian-American Press and Information Center. The Center is a project of New York University's Center for War, Peace and the News Media. This essay was translated by Conrad Hohenlohe.

9

Defiant Publishing in Nigeria

Dapo Olorunyomi

In June 1995 in Nigeria, the despotic regime of Gen. Sani Abacha sentenced to jail four editors—Kunle Ajibade, Charles Obi, George Mbah and Christine Anyanwu—after accusing them of conspiring to overthrow his martial order. Hardly had these editors begun to serve their 15-year terms when, in December of the same year, another editor, Nosa Igiebor, was arrested and jailed—this time without any charge against him and no benefit of a trial. Was it a coincidence that all these editors practiced within the tradition of the newsmagazine genre? No.

In a significant sense, the history of the latter half of the 1980s in Nigeria is the history of press-military conflict. If Nigerians continue to invest an abiding faith in the press, it is partly because the press has always represented a vital matrix for their civil society, going back to the 19th century when Lagos newspapers argued for democracy and independence. In our own time, the press became one of the first institutions to wrestle for its freedom and engage the dictatorship in low-intensity internal warfare by reinventing dissent through a return to the investigative tradition. This movement was led by the newsmagazines. Their struggles made the 10 years of 1985 to 1995 the most exciting phase of Nigerian journalism since those heroic days in the 19th century.

In 1985, the military in Nigeria was already marking two decades of a legal monopoly of power, during which its main concern had been to centralize politics and the economy and to pave the way for the strengthening of executive power, so that a tiny technocratic elite, working in alliance with a political segment of the armed forces, could impose an authoritarian vision on the whole of Nigerian society. The first casualty of this effort would be Nigerian federalism; after a succession of setbacks, it would climax in the final dismemberment of the civil order.

This effort took place in the context of economic stagnation, punctuated by resuscitative measures that inflicted hardships on the middle class and urban and rural working people. Predictably, as social tension systematically increased, human rights abuses became a logical recourse for the regime.

Repression was not new in Africa, nor in Nigeria. But the new dictatorship, headed by Gen. Ibrahim Babangida, set out on a fascinating if not doomed experiment in an international environment characterized by Mikhail Gorbachev's *glasnost* and *perestroika*. The issue was simple: Can a dictatorship survive in an age of democratization?

Spurred on by the belief, famous during the Cold War, that "dictatorship is good for business," the authoritarian order in Nigeria attempted to answer "yes." It also basked in the illusion that it was the only institution with a monopoly over legitimate violence and that it could generate some kind of coherent regime.

The government also nursed the vision that it could deploy force to do "what is right." After brutally suppressing a civil protest of the urban poor and students in 1986 at the height of the resistance to a Structural Adjustment Program, Babangida himself boasted: "We are masters in the art of management of internal violence."

While excluding class organizations (though not class interests) from decision-making, the Babangida government managed to ensure a link between civil society and the regime by an ideology of co-optation. Individuals and groups like the press and labor were brought into a power circle that was rigidly controlled by security agencies and military commanders.

This plan to dismantle civil society had a profound implication for the press in particular. By quickly "co-opting" a significant section of the "leadership" of the press into its agenda of "saving the society from collapse" and by abrogating a decree from the previous regime that rendered journalists vulnerable to prosecution, the dictatorship hoodwinked a large section of the civil society into its brigade and helped to show the lack of character in a large section of the Nigerian elite.

The press would pay dearly for its own myopia. In 1986, one of the most flamboyant editors in the history of the Nigerian press, Dele Giwa, was blown off his breakfast table by a parcel bomb believed to have been sent by government security agents. Newspaper closings and the detention of journalists became the norm. Employing a mix of corruption, bribery and outright coercion, the Babangida dictatorship suppressed civil society and the judiciary, which was rendered prostrate by a series of ouster clauses, retroactive legislation and a growing wave of executive lawlessness.

With the repression of the press growing day by day, with the absence of any civil institution of social mobilization and with the added monopoly of radio and television at the behest of the regime, the morphology of the civil society, of which the press is a crucial segment, took on a disturbing new meaning. Would the dictatorship subdue the institution of the newspaper press that, since its founding in 1859, had built a strong, heroic, independent and pro-democratic tradition?

The return of the investigative tradition to Nigerian journalism challenged the military's sense of its own legitimacy. It bitterly reminded the martial order that in opposition to its "presumptive legitimacy" was a "presumptive parliament" of journalism. Indeed, the independent press of the latter half of the 1980s truly represented the first self-actualizing, consistent and articulate "surrogate parliament" in the history of the subdued civil order in Nigeria.

Unhappily, given the limits of the spoken and written word, this "surrogate parliament" was not always positioned to win. Yet the "power of the word," with all its limitations, remains the only medium for extracting accountability, good governance and openness in government under the present corrupt and ruthless dictatorship.

Since the collapse of Babangida's dictatorship under economic and political pressure and the relay of power to Gen. Abacha in 1993, the military has scored a string of straight As in its repression of the press. Nowhere in Africa, contrary to the vain claims of the regime, is the press assailed and persecuted as in Nigeria. Repression comes in many styles and patterns: detention without trial, imprisonment without due process, constant security and police visitation to newspaper houses, frequent "invitations" to journalists and editors for security questioning, proscription of critical newspapers and journals, arson against opposition newspapers, assassinations or attempts, death threats against investigative journalists or courageous newspaper commentators, massive product seizure so as to bankrupt newspapers, harassment and intimidation of vendors selling anti-government newspapers, telephone- and fax-line bugging of newspapers and news managers, travel restrictions, counterfeiting opposition newspapers to discredit them, smear campaigns against journalists, bribery and infiltration of media ranks to stain their credibility.

The intensive repression of the press in the late 1980s occurred as newsmagazines proliferated. Indeed, it was designed to nullify them and other media. Regular newspapers made salutary contributions to the cause of freedom and were also victims of random and ruthless repression, but the magazines suffered the most in human and material terms.

As the foster child of a new global sensibility that fructified in the collapse of the Berlin Wall, the very possibility of the press becoming a presumptive parliament in Nigeria owed its evolution to the yoking of two factors never discussed before now: an American-style tradition of investigative reporting seen in the 1985 founding of *Newswatch* magazine and the entrance into the profession of a well-educated and politically committed crop of reporters. Not only were these young men and women prowling their beats with the confidence of brilliant college graduates, they had also undergone an activist baptism of fire from the anti-apartheid and student movements.

These two factors dovetailed perfectly with the needs of the already troubled Nigerian middle class, the major consumers of the printed word, who demanded a new information and analytical compass to grapple with an increasingly complex global experience.

If the traditional readership class was content to consume "unmediated" news and entertainment, the new elite expected a modicum of editorial torch bearing to light the paths of a new and treacherous world. Suddenly, the sun was setting for the reporter as a jack-of-all-trades. The white-collar journalist with specialized training in finance, politics, human rights, aviation or even the delightful study of the stars was coming into prominence.

By promising to deliver the breadth and depth of news (and analysis) in a seductive and elegant style, while also advancing the claim that readers could save money now by buying fewer of the regular daily newspapers, the newsmagazine correctly defined its audience—the Nigerian middle class.

But was this not the same class that provided the technical platform, as economic consultants, to counterbalance the crude ethics of the ruling soldiers? And would the commitment of the regime to deactivate the middle segment and popular sector of the society through its political and economic exclusion programs not ultimately destroy this class?

In their consistent proposal of a moral and political alternative to the ossified vision of the regime, since 1985 the magazines—which functioned in collaboration with human rights bodies and organizations in the political opposition—became institutional enemy No. 1. The regime marked them for destruction. Newsmagazines, and their allies, argued that since the regime (and the military as a whole) presided over Nigeria's economic collapse, social instability and abortion of democracy, neither Abacha nor any military dispensation could lead the nation to recovery or democracy. In the binary mind-set of the dictatorship, this was treason. The totalitarian Abacha regime responded with the conviction of the four editors last June, the ongoing war against the media and a desperate campaign against the so-called imperialism of the Western media.

There are strong indications that the regime will soon roll out a new law to create a media registration agency that prescribes new and draconian guidelines to regulate the independent press. Under the new law, actually only a refurbished version of the controversial "Decree No. 43" of 1993, the independent press is characterized as a "source of incitement to civil war and physical disintegration" of Nigeria!

Resistance to these acts of repression has, however, developed in arithmetic progression. The year 1993 stood out: The regime issued four decrees (Nos. 33, 35, 43 and 48) to control the independent press, and seven media houses suffered from an unprecedented clamp-down in July, a move now known as the "Great Shutdown."

One of the profound ironies of the '90s is that state brutality, as intense as it was, failed to completely drive the independent press under. Against all odds, the novelty of "defiant publishing" was inaugurated in 1993. An era of "defiant broadcasting" came into being in 1995 with a pirate radio, the Freedom Frequency Radio (F&F), emerging to challenge the state monopoly of the airwaves. A third dimension of the acts of defiance was the flurry of litigation brought against the regime to reveal its inherently lawless nature. Not surprisingly, in all the cases brought against the government, the court ruled in favor of the media—Nigeria has one of the most independent judiciaries in the Commonwealth. But the government disregarded the court's decision.

While "private radio" could broadcast for only an hour a day and only occasionally on the FM band, the phenomenon of defiant publishing, otherwise dubbed "guerrilla journalism," was a much more revolutionary event. In May 1993, when the regime proscribed *The News* magazine, its managers, in a courageous act of dissent, quietly floated an alternative paper, *Tempo,* to operate underground. So electrifying and dazzling was this experience that it rendered the security institutions dumb and helpless. For the civil society, it vividly illustrated the power of information in the assault against a decadent dictatorship. So paranoid was the regime that it started arresting people caught reading either *The News* or *Tempo*. Such was the case on June 25, 1993, when four men were arrested at the Federal Secretariat in Min, Niger State, for allegedly buying and reading Xerox copies of *The News*!

The notion of a newsroom was transformed from a regular static setting into a dynamic, on-the-wheel experience. At normal times *The News* usually structures its week into two parts, a three-day editorial segment and a three-day production segment. The editorial segment requires that the three departments of the paper ("Back of the Book," "Business and Economy" and "Nation and Politics") meet to generate and discuss story ideas every Sunday in the newsroom. Bureau staff were expected to send in their stories before Sunday to a senior editor. A late Monday meeting of line editors would broaden and deepen the perspectives of the stories, especially the cover choices. That also required a newsroom setting. The production segment, which was basically an editing and postediting part of the job, also required a regular office setting, all of which assumed a proximity to a library, a telephone and fax machine. All these were turned around in the context of guerrilla journalism, and reporters and editors, constantly on the move, had to write, edit and publish clandestinely in surreptitious locations.

Between May and November 1993, week after week without fail, *Tempo* hit the streets. After a frustrating but futile attempt to halt the paper or apprehend its editors, the government declared that it could only have been published inside the American Embassy! The truth was that it was published in a private, nondescript office, a few blocks from Nigerian police headquarters!

Places like stadiums and theaters became the "newsrooms" where a highly decentralized structure allowed each department of the magazine to meet in groups of six under a disguised framework. Watch those soccer spectators well—six men in the crowd are redefining the newsroom idea! Watch that yoga group at the gym—are they discussing story ideas under the guise of meditation? Watch that small group sitting under the tree near the theater waiting for the movie to open—are these not guerrilla journalists!

Tempo set an example of defiant publishing under a ruthless dictatorship, but the costs were enormous. The government was unable to catch up with me, so my wife and three-month-old baby were arrested in 1993. A vendor selling *Tempo* was struck and killed by a fast-moving car as he was escaping from the police. Revenue returns on circulation became slow and irregular, deeply hurting the publishing effort. Editors had to maintain a status of strict internal exile, and for about six months I could not stay in my home. I hopped from one sleeping hole to another every night, moving about in crowded commuter buses to evade arrest. But the collapse of the Babangida regime on Aug. 26, 1993, was partly attributed to the efforts of the independent press. For the guerrilla publications, it was a golden moment.

The fact that *Tell* magazine in Nigeria also published underground in a quasi-guerrilla status for much of 1996 suggests the growing popularity of defiant publishing as a tool of combat against a repressive regime and an index of collective will serving as the carrier of demands for substantive justice toward the poorer segment of the population. Sadly, however, authoritarianism continues to prosper in Nigeria.

Nigeria is now a country that has seen the ethnic cleansing of Ogoniland, where a man who won a presidential mandate of 14 million votes ended up in jail because he would not deal with the regime, and where his wife, fighting for his release, was brutally assassinated; and where the list of assassinated political opponents of the ruling regime grows daily—as does the detention of human right activists and journalists. Nigerians are fleeing into exile, some on economic grounds, but many for political reasons: This has become a painful prelude to the chaos that is yet to come.

The press, therefore, has an added, though not necessarily new, challenge—a challenge made urgent with the low capacity for the formation of public opinion, the overbearing presence of executive lawlessness and the determination of the regime to impose "tacit" consensus by blood and fire. The press must draw from its illustrious tradition of 19th-century Lagos to remain as a redoubtable surrogate parliament. While the sheer magnitude of the mess in Nigeria and the dangerous prospects of defiant publishing make an absolute victory impossible, the press has no choice but to continue to push the government to keep clear in its mind that the age of guns and jackboots, having become absolutely anachronistic, will soon pass.

Dapo Olorunyomi edited The News *and* Tempo *magazines in Nigeria until March of 1996 when he was forced into exile. In April, he was awarded the International Editor of the Year Award by the* World Press Review, *and in October he received the 1996 Freedom-to-Write Award from PEN Center USA West.*

10

Indonesia—Cracks in the Wall

Vikram A. Parekh

Can a nation that has tasted freedom of the press be forced back into censorship and the imprisonment of independent journalists? Indonesia may well offer an answer.

Since winning independence from the Dutch in 1949, the vast and populous southeast Asian nation has been dominated by two successive rulers: Sukarno, a charismatic, if at times autocratic, nationalist of leftist leanings who led the independence struggle, and Suharto, a dictatorial general. Suharto took power in 1967 after the suppression of a 1965 coup attempt that triggered the brutal persecution—which took hundreds of thousands of lives—of the legally constituted Indonesian Communist Party. President Suharto's regime has been characterized by authoritarian rule, an adherence to free-market economics that has fostered a substantial middle class and a brief interlude of relative press freedom.

Six years ago, Suharto announced a new policy of *keterbukaan,* or openness, in response to mounting pressure from local nongovernmental organizations, international human rights groups and foreign governments. It also served to defuse a growing rift between Suharto and Indonesia's powerful army, which had expressed dissatisfaction with his authoritarianism.

Local journalists seized the opportunity and injected critical and investigative voices into the country's previously staid media. New publications appeared, including the weekly tabloids *Editor* and *DeTik,* which pushed the margins of independent journalism.

DeTik offered perhaps the most dramatic testimony to the political sophistication of Indonesian readers. Introduced in February 1993, its courageous style of reporting—previously encountered only in underground journals—boosted circulation in the space of a year from 7,000 to more than 450,000 copies. *DeTik* was brave, intelligent and profitable.

The weeklies printed dissenting commentary, covered political scandals—including a controversial warship purchase—and reported on labor and ethnic unrest. They depicted a country racked by cronyism, corruption and civil disturbance—the very traits likely to scare away investors in the country's fast-growing economy. By reporting on separatist movements in Aceh and East Timor, they belied the regime's pretense of control over the archipelago's far-flung islands.

Appearing when many were beginning to question the country's prospects after the demise of the 75-year-old Suharto, *DeTik* and its contemporaries rattled the government. In June 1994, *DeTik,* along with *Editor* and *Tempo*—the country's largest-circulation glossy newsmagazine and the pioneer of independent journalism in the mainstream press—was banned by the Information Ministry.

Indonesian newsstands now feature two publications intended by the Suharto regime to serve as replacements: *Gatra,* a glossy pro-government newsmagazine owned by Suharto crony Muhammad "Bob" Hassan, and the similarly acquiescent tabloid *Tiras,* owned by Minister of Manpower Abdul Latief. Other publications that once tested the limits of *keterbukaan* have dramatically curtailed the extent of their investigative reporting.

The reaction to the press bans revealed that *keterbukaan* had changed Indonesians' expectations of the media. In the weeks that followed the banning, cities throughout Indonesia witnessed demonstrations by journalists, activists and most importantly, ordinary readers. The demonstrations reflected in part the emergence of a new generation of reporters and editors—journalists accustomed to reporting with restraints that were more akin to leashes than straitjackets.

The depth of popular support for the weeklies caught many journalists by surprise. In an essay about the banning, Indonesian free-lancer and activist Rachlan Nashidik pointed to a broader discontent that underlay the demonstrations:

> We will not certainly forget the time *Tempo* revealed the mass killing in Jakarta's Tanjung Priok, the mysterious murder of [labor activist] Marsinha, the arrest and imprisonment of Nuku Soleiman and the 21 students who dared to criticize the president.... people are angry, they do not want to live under the dominance of a regime which does everything without any shame to keep its hold on its own tyrannical power.

The public protests subsided after brutal assaults by Indonesian police and military forces, but Indonesian journalists' efforts to defend their rights continued. Many who had worked for the banned publications, or who had taken part in the demonstrations against their closure, were incensed by the reaction of the state-sponsored Indonesian Journalists' Association (PWI), which issued a statement saying it "understood" the reasons for the bans.

After meeting in the West Java town of Sirnagalih in August 1994, over 50 journalists announced the formation of the country's only independent press union: the Alliance of Independent Journalists (AJI).

Since its inception, AJI has dramatically challenged the regime's press curbs. Among AJI's first actions was to publish a book of essays by prominent Indonesian journalists on the impact of the June 1994 press bans. To reach both international and Indonesian audiences, the book was published in English and Bahasa Indonesia, the country's national language. Next, AJI began an even more daring venture: the publication of a newsmagazine that would fill the void in investigative reporting left by *Tempo, DeTik,* and *Editor.*

Entitled *Independen,* the monthly magazine debuted in the fall of 1994 and quickly drew an audience well beyond its circulation of about 10,000 copies. Its articles covered topics such as the personal wealth of government ministers, the successor to Suharto and nepotism in Suharto's inner circle.

But *Independen* did not have a publishing license and stood no chance of getting one. Under Indonesian law only press corporations may publish, and those corporations must secure publishing licenses from the Information Ministry.

Under the licensing process, the Information Ministry has the authority to approve the mandate and editorship of each publication. These provisions give the Ministry wide latitude to deny and revoke licenses. Of the three banned weeklies, for example, two officially lost their licenses for technical infractions: *DeTik* for deviating from its stated mission of publishing crime reports and *Editor* for failing to inform the Ministry of personnel changes in its editorial board.

There was a more insidious consequence of the licensing regime, according to an article in *Independen*: by abusing his authority to grant permits, Information Minister Harmoko had amassed substantial shares in the country's largest press corporations. AJI members believe that it was this report, more than any other, that prompted authorities to increase pressure on *Independen.*

In March 1995, police raided an AJI function and arrested its president, Ahmad Taufik, as well as several other union members. They also detained Danang Kukuh Wardoyo, AJI's 19-year-old office assistant. Later that evening, about 20 police officers raided AJI's office, arrested AJI member Eko Maryadi and seized the group's computers, fax machine and files.

A three-month trial began in June 1995. Taufik and Maryadi were charged with violating Article 19 of the press law, which prohibits the publication of an unlicensed newspaper or magazine, and Article 154 of the criminal code, which bars the expression of "feelings of hostility, hatred or contempt toward the government."

The case attracted massive attention in Indonesia, neighboring countries such as Australia and the international human rights community. The British freedom of expression group Article 19 sent an observer to the trial, while the New York-based Committee to Protect Journalists (CPJ) conferred one of its prestigious annual press freedom awards on Taufik. The most remarkable demonstration of support came from Indonesians themselves, who packed the courtroom for each session and openly denounced the verdict: 32 months in prison each. Wardoyo received a jail term of 18 months for his role in distributing *Independen*.

International opprobrium and domestic outrage followed, but the Suharto regime proved impervious to both—an indication that it was determined to maintain control over the media at all costs. The 32-month prison terms handed down to Taufik and Maryadi were actually extended on appeal to three years in prison each. And last March, the Indonesian Supreme Court upheld that decision, limiting the two journalists' options within the judicial system to a review by the same court.

Taufik and Maryadi still continued to write, sending letters to three publications about conditions in Cipinang prison and interviewing a fellow prisoner, East Timorese leader Jose Alexandre "Xanana" Gusmao, for *Independen*.

On Aug. 16, authorities responded by transferring them to a remote facility in Cirebon, 200 kilometers east of Jakarta.

But Taufik and Maryadi have not been the only members of AJI to bear the fallout of the government's crackdown on the union. By law, all working journalists in Indonesia must be members of the state-sponsored PWI. Although the requirement was often disregarded in the past, in the wake of AJI's formation authorities announced that it would henceforth be strictly enforced. In effect, journalists involved with AJI were blacklisted.

When *DeTik*'s publishers tried to revive the tabloid under the name *Simponi,* in October 1994, they were forced to close after one issue because their staff included non-PWI members. Simultaneous membership in the two press unions became impossible after March 1995, when PWI expelled 13 of its members for having signed the Sirnagalih Declaration establishing AJI. Among them were Goenawan Mohamad, the internationally respected editor and publisher of *Tempo,* and Eros Djarot, the editor who had spearheaded *DeTik*'s move into investigative journalism.

Through direct pressure on editors and publishers, over 80 AJI members have been forced out of their jobs, while others have been demoted or shunted to dead-end assignments. AJI spokesperson Andreas Harsono, for example, was fired from his job at the *Jakarta Post* in October 1994 because he was deemed "unsuitable." Harsono's dismissal came just two weeks after a PWI-sponsored meeting at which *Jakarta Post* editor Santoso Pudjomartono reportedly pledged to take firm measures against AJI members on his staff.

Despite the repression, AJI members and many other Indonesian journalists continue to circumvent official media constraints. *Tempo* magazine, which last May lost a court battle to have its publishing license restored, is available in an Internet edition. However, its reach is limited to Indonesia's intelligentsia and falls far short of the print edition's circulation of 190,000.

Several former *Tempo* journalists have established a firm that produces the Sunday edition of the newspaper *Media Indonesia* on contract. In the year since its debut, the Sunday paper has earned a reputation among Indonesian readers as one of the most editorially independent publications among the licensed media.

Media Indonesia, however, has had its own brushes with the authorities. Last September, its directors suspended publication of the Sunday edition for four weeks. The announcement came shortly after the Sunday paper ran an interview with Islamic scholar Nurcholish Madjid, in which he criticized the country's political system and called for the creation of new opposition parties. Although the Information Ministry denied involvement in the decision to suspend the publication, few in the Indonesian press community saw it as anything other than a reaction to official pressure.

The same month saw other Indonesian media sustain casualties for airing the views of well-known political dissidents. A popular weekly television show, "Perspektif," was canceled five days after it broadcast a segment that featured the veteran independent journalist Mochtar Lubis as a guest. And the Sumatra-based newspaper *Lampung Post* suspended four of its reporters after receiving an official complaint about an interview with Indonesia's most celebrated novelist, Pramoedya Ananta Toer, who lives under house arrest.

The depth of discontent with the present order in Indonesia was revealed very recently. In July 1996, Jakarta was engulfed by riots set off by the army's seizure of Indonesian Democratic Party (PDI) headquarters from loyalists of the party's ousted leader, Megawati Sukarnoputri, Sukarno's daughter, who had advocated a freer political system for Indonesia.

Outraged citizens took to the streets. Demonstrations, which drew upwards of 50,000 protesters, spun wildly out of control. Office buildings and small businesses alike were set ablaze. The riots were quelled as the army deployed tanks and troops throughout Jakarta, a move that presaged the sweeping arrests of students, labor activists and opposition figures. However misplaced the rioters' targets may at times have been, their rage indicated both the depth of discontent with the prevailing autocracy and the deafening lack of outlets for freedom of expression.

The prospects for press freedom in Indonesia are still uncertain. But Indonesian journalists who attempt to navigate these tortuous straits are armed with a legacy of independent journalism and a readership that is prepared to demand it. However limited the floodgate that Suharto opened six years ago, the fact remains that Indonesia's media and the reading public were transformed. Now the movement is theirs, and the setbacks that Suharto imposes can in the end be only temporary.

Vikram A. Parekh is a research associate at Human Rights Watch.

11

The Long Arm of British Law

Geoffrey Robertson

The sun may have set on the British Empire, but not on English common law principles that infringe upon freedom of expression.

Among the former colonies, the United States, with its First Amendment, bars their application—a considerable achievement. But other nations, whose freedom has been grudgingly granted rather than won by revolution, are less fortunate. Independence has come with strings of repressive common law attached to it, strings that political leaders pull to the discomfit of journalists and political dissidents alike.

True, Britain today presents a benign enough country for free speech. This is partly because its more oppressive laws are left unused, or have been ameliorated by the influence of the European Convention on Human Rights, whose court in Strasbourg, France, has forced many overdue reforms.

But the British press remains intimidated by heavy fines and damages for contempt of court and defamation. Indeed, London is the libel capital of the world, attracting forum-shopping foreign plaintiffs to sue in order to restore reputations they cannot protect in their own countries.

In Britain, libel remains a tort of strict liability, and the burden of proving any defense rests on the media defendant. As some American newspapers have discovered to their cost, English courts accept jurisdiction if just one copy is published within the country, and free speech can prove exceedingly expensive.

But the problems of defending speech under English law grow the further the case is from England. There may be few British colonies left, but there are no less than 48 independent nations, members of the British Commonwealth, which have had bequeathed to them British common law and legislation, without the antidote of a First Amendment or the corrective of a European Court of Human Rights.

Sixteen Commonwealth nations still have, as their final court of appeal, the Privy Council, composed of senior British judges sitting in a court adjacent to the Downing Street residence of the prime minister. The other countries that have inherited these laws may change them—judges have to some extent done so in Australia and Canada—but in most cases find them very convenient as a means of stifling dissent and limiting public criticism. They are not pejoratively perceived as "colonial" laws—quite the contrary. They are defended as the inheritance of a stable and civilized society.

British libel law has great attractions for politicians throughout the Commonwealth. As prime minister of Singapore, Lee Kuan Yew bankrupted opposition members of Parliament by suing them for speeches they made on the hustings, and any criticism of the judges was punished by prosecutions for the arcane offense of "scandalising the judiciary." Powerful figures in Malaysia, too, have recently won massive financial awards against journalists: absent a "public figure" defense, the very prospect of such an action can be intimidating.

More serious, perhaps, is the common law relating to seditious libel, which makes it a criminal offense to stir up anger against the government or between "different classes of citizen." Dr. Hastings Kamuzu Banda, former president-for-life in Malawi, used this offense to jail opponents in the years before his overthrow. It is still much in evidence (together with the common law crime of treason) in prosecutions of journalists and opposition figures in Kenya and Ghana.

One inheritance from the dying days of colonialism that has frequently been deployed is "emergency" legislation—typically laws left on the books long after the emergency has passed—enabling the detention of "subversives" without trial. Such regulations come replete with English case law, which may be quoted and followed in Commonwealth courts, and which generally supports the powers in question. They are found not only in Commonwealth countries, but in nations once touched by British rule. The 1945 Defence Regulations imposed during British rule in Palestine, for example, were incorporated into Israeli law after independence. They permit official censorship and the detention of journalists, and have never been repealed.

A Cabinet Minister once described secrecy as "the British disease," and it is in developing laws to protect officialdom that the country has excelled. It was not until 1995 that the government was prepared to admit that MI6 (the British equivalent of the CIA) even existed. Until 1989, the Official Secrets Act made it an offense punishable by two years' imprisonment for a journalist to reveal the menu in the Department of Defence canteen, and the government can still suppress any mention of a subject by issuing what is called a "D notice" to the media. These laws are found, usually unreformed, in all Commonwealth countries. They provide a ready basis (with little or no defense) for prosecuting journalists and editors who publish "leaked" information.

The problem is one of principle. English law has little concept of the dangers of prior restraint. Lacking any constitutional protection for human rights, it has developed essentially in order to protect property, including property in information, at the behest of government or powerful private litigants. Injunctions against publication of "confidential" information are regularly granted, and demands for freedom of information acts are still positively resisted.

Lawyers from the Commonwealth, trained in traditional English law, often unthinkingly adopt its philosophy. Thus Mrs. Thatcher was advised that she could stop publication of *Spycatcher* (an account of low doings in the British domestic intelligence service MI5) throughout the former Empire—with the exception of the United States. And she succeeded in a number of countries, until judges in Australia were finally prepared to call her bluff.

There are many arcane laws, once used regularly in Britain, that may be expedient for governments in modern times. The law against blasphemous libel, for example, has recently been invoked to ban books and endanger authors in Pakistan and Bangladesh. The law of criminal libel was invoked recently in Uganda to prosecute a journalist who had asked Kenneth Kaunda, longtime president of Zambia, whether he was not too old to lead his country. It is possible to go to jail for "contempt of Parliament" (a crime tried and punished by politicians themselves) or for "incitement to disaffection" by promoting pacifism.

What is so alarming about the array of colonial laws is not that they are used, but that there is no impetus to repeal or reform them. Governments want to keep them—just in case—and judges lack the power to strike them down. Although many Commonwealth countries do have bills of rights, these were drafted and imposed by the British government on the granting of independence. Their promises of "freedom of expression" are invariably subject to the qualification that they do not affect laws existing at the time. Governments that wish to curb freedom of expression cannot pass new laws to do so—but then they do not need to, because the old British laws are ample for their purposes.

There has been one recent exception. In Hong Kong, the democratically elected legislative council decided last year to repeal a number of colonial ordinances, for fear of their misuse by the incoming Chinese administration. But China has now announced that it will reintroduce these laws. If freedom of speech becomes imperiled in Hong Kong, it will not be under some new Chinese *diktat*. It will be done according to the book, by prosecutions for criminal or seditious libel, or for contempt of court or breaches of official secrecy.

Britain no longer rules the waves, but in countries throughout the world it is the British rule book that tends to be waved at journalists and authors, in an edition much more strict than applies in Britain. The Commonwealth is a loose political association that meets regularly to make noises about breaches of human rights. But it has never scrutinized its own legal legacy, much less established a court that could require the repeal or reform of colonial laws infringing on the Universal Declaration of Human Rights. Until it does, the built-in bias against freedom of expression, despite piecemeal reform in a few Commonwealth countries, will remain in the laws of too many lands.

Geoffrey Robertson, QC, a barrister in London, has been involved in many high profile media cases involving the protection of journalists and their sources. He is author of Media Law *(1992) and* Freedom, the Individual and the Law *(1993).*

12

Turkish Journalists on Trial

Ahmet Emin

A Turkish villager writes to his uncle in Istanbul: "Dear uncle, you have been living in the big city for a long time. You must know a lot of people by now. Perhaps you can arrange a simple job for me so I can move there. I'll be anything—doorman, porter, street vendor..."

His uncle replies: "Dear nephew, Yes, I can get you a job easily. But forget about being a porter or doorman—such jobs are very hard to get here. However, would you like to be a responsible editor for a newspaper?"

This anecdote from a 1990 story by the late Aziz Nesin, a famous Turkish author, is not meant to demean Turkish newspaper editors. It was written to point at difficulties they face: "Responsible editors" are recruited to fill in for others who are imprisoned for writings that appear in their paper. While they serve time in jail, another editor is found to take responsibility and then face a new prison sentence.

Nesin's story, a satire, ridicules something that happens frequently in Turkey: the punishment of editors by legal means for publishing unorthodox writings. Using an array of broad and vague laws, Turkish authorities jail and fine thousands of journalists and shut down dozens of papers, magazines and television stations.

While their colleagues around the world face harassment from thugs, physical attacks, assassinations, extralegal pressure from police and outright censorship, Turkish journalists are intimidated and censored under laws which, at first glance, seem friendly to press freedom. The 28th Article of the Turkish Constitution begins, "The press is free and shall not be censored." While this first sentence makes you think all is fine, the rest of the article is a long list of exceptions. Press freedom does not exist for "anyone who writes or prints any news or articles which threaten the internal or external security of the state or the indivisible integrity of the state with its territory and nation, which tend to incite offense, riot or insurrection, or which refer to classified State secrets and anyone who..." the list goes on for half a page.

Moreover, Turkey even has a special branch of prosecutors who deal solely with the press. They read every little publication printed every day looking for things against the law—or the interests of the state.

Altogether, according to the prestigious daily *Cumhuriyet* (The Republic), in some 160 laws there are close to 800 clauses that are used to restrict what the press can say. At the end of 1995, *Cumhuriyet* reported recently, there were 136 writers, journalists, politicians and intellectuals imprisoned for their views. According to the Committee to Protect Journalists (CPJ), an international press freedom group based in New York, 51 of these were journalists—editors, reporters and columnists jailed for their writings. For the second year in a row, Turkey led the world in the number of journalists it jailed, CPJ's annual report said.

Although this all sounds very dismal, it would be wrong to presume there is no press freedom in Turkey. As long as they leave a handful of taboo subjects alone, Turkish journalists are pretty much free to write whatever they wish. But touching those taboo issues means legal trouble.

The biggest taboo subject is the 12-year-old Kurdish insurgency in the country's southeast. The conflict, which first started as an independence movement but later turned into a fight for cultural rights and political autonomy, has claimed more than 20,000 lives. Until recently, Kurds were banned from even speaking their language, publishing or making music in it. Broadcasting and education in Kurdish are still not permitted.

The "unity" of Turkey is an obsession of the Turkish government. Its position on the Kurdish insurgency is that a small group of terrorists wants to divide up Turkey. The government says that it will not allow that and pledges to destroy the terrorists and refuses to talk to ruthless killers. Anyone who says anything different is viewed as a supporter of "separatist terrorists."

It is very tricky for journalists to write about the Kurdish conflict because the publication of anything the government deems to serve the interests of "separatists" will result in legal trouble. Pure reporting about clashes between Kurdish guerrillas and Turkish forces can be, and often is, seen as "separatist" if it reports human rights abuses by security forces. Columnists advocating peace are frequently sentenced to prison for separatism because they might be calling for negotiations with the rebels.

For a long time, the most popular law used to punish unorthodox views on the Kurdish conflict was Article 8 of the so-called Anti-Terror Law. It was softened last December under pressure from the European Union, just before the organization was about to vote on a favorable trade agreement with Turkey. The Turkish government, eager for approval, revised Article 8 slightly. It still punishes any writing that "endangers the indivisibility of the state"—an undefined concept that can be interpreted as liberally as the court pleases—but the article is no longer as popular as it once was among "press prosecutors."

The most popular law used by press prosecutors today is Article 312 of the penal code, which punishes "inciting racial enmity." The law's breadth and scope allow it to be used against any kind of writing. Many times prosecutors have cited passages similar to the following in "offending newspapers" to establish convictions under Article 312: "The Kurdish and Turkish people should live in peace and harmony." The prosecutorial rationale is that identifying two ethnically different peoples incites hatred and division.

You might be tempted to ask, "Doesn't the Turkish government recognize the existence of Kurds?" It does. Everybody does. But the above sentence is used against pro-Kurdish and left-wing publications while mainstream media and politicians say the same thing all the time without getting into trouble. That's because the mainstream media refuse to stray from the official view on the Kurdish conflict. They do not report any human rights abuses related to the Kurdish war and confine themselves to publishing the military's statements about clashes.

It wasn't always like this. Just four or five years ago, the Turkish press covered the Kurdish conflict extensively. Reporters went to the scene and covered human rights abuses committed by both sides. Interviews with Kurdish rebel leaders and visits to their camps were regular features.

This was not an easy way of life for reporters, however. Journalists faced physical threats: They were shot at during battle and harassed physically by both sides. Kidnappings were frequent. In 1992, Turkey led the world in the killing of journalists, with 11 murders.

But the press was not intimidated. So the government resorted to legal methods, and they worked.

Faced with trials over their writings, the mainstream media started dropping their coverage of the conflict. Over the years, they perfected the art of self-censorship. Gradually, they even bought the government's argument that the "unity of the country is in danger" and started defending it with fervor. All this happened while the Kurdish rebels scaled down their demands from independence to autonomy.

The alternative press, which was unwilling to censor itself, suffered continued and vigorous punishment. Turkey's only pro-Kurdish daily has had to change its name four times since 1992, once for each time it was shut down for publishing "separatist" stories. A score of its responsible editors served jail time; a few remain imprisoned.

According to CPJ's 1994 report, 329 trials were launched in connection with writings appearing in *Ozgur Ulke,* the pro-Kurdish daily's 1994 incarnation. Even *Ozgur Ulke*'s lawyers could not keep track of the total number of years its editors received in prison. And out of 234 publishing days, authorities confiscated *Ozgur Ulke* on all but five of them.

Until 1995, confiscation had little effect. The press law bans "prior restraint" and allows confiscation of a publication only after authorities have read what is published. Prosecutors could order dailies to be confiscated the day they came out, but because by then they would be distributed throughout the country and bought by readers, the orders did not carry the weight of "censorship." The subsequent trials and the sentences received were the real burden—thus the rotating editors.

But in 1995, the hardworking press prosecutors found a way around the law. They would send a police officer to the printing plant early in the evening when the national editions were being printed. The police would get a copy of the early edition hot off the press and rush it back to the prosecutor, who would immediately issue a confiscation order. The confiscation orders were preprinted, with blanks left for the titles of stories deemed in violation of the laws.

The police could confiscate the paper as it came off the press, preventing it from reaching readers. Faced with this new method, the alternative press adapted: After they handed a copy of the early edition to the police, they would stop the presses and wait for the confiscation order. The police who arrived with the order would be given the 100 or so copies printed, the articles cited in the order would be wiped out from the negatives, and the paper rerun with white blank spaces but without anything "illegal." In effect, they traded the opportunity to run their "most illegal" stories for the opportunity to reach people with the rest of their publication. So that no one would mistake the effect of censorship, they would print the word "censored" in the blank spaces.

So while Turkish laws prohibited censorship, Turkish prosecutors managed to become censors. The pro-Kurdish daily, after its third closure in August 1995, learned the lesson that mainstream Turkish media learned a while ago. The fourth incarnation was much milder—no criticism of the government crackdown against Kurdish rebels, no independent reporting of the conflict and no terms, like *Kurdistan,* that angered the authorities.

Demokrasi, the newest pro-Kurdish paper, is no longer censored daily. Its editors face only a handful of trials, not hundreds. The government has won. Some truly radical left-wing weeklies, still unwilling to bend, receive harsh treatment. But the important, higher-circulation alternative press has obeyed.

Besides the Kurdish insurgency, a few other issues are off-limits for journalists if they want to stay out of legal trouble. To criticize Mustafa Kemal Ataturk, the long-dead founder of modern Turkey, is not allowed. Ataturk is revered by most Turks, especially among the governing elite, and to criticize his views or deeds, or suggest that he even once did something wrong, is punishable with a prison sentence.

Nor can the military, always a major force in Turkish politics and society, be criticized. The generals have taken over the government three times since 1960 and remain an untouchable institution. All Turkish men have to serve in the military, and conscientious objectors are seen as traitors. Journalists who wrote about draft resisters have been court-martialed for "attempting to discourage military service." Turkey is probably the only country where civilians are court-martialed for their purely civilian acts.

Another touchy subject is the secular structure of Turkey. While both authorities and the Western-oriented majority see secularism as a basic pillar of society, there is a growing Islamist movement that has questioned that assumption. But openly denouncing secularism in print is against the law. Radical Islamist papers have been the target of legal action, although not as heavily as the left-wing and pro-Kurdish publications.

However, the ascension of an Islamist party to power this year will most likely change the attitude of the courts toward this issue. Although the government has always claimed that Turkey's courts are fully independent, and has used that as an excuse that it has no control over the judiciary's prosecution of journalists, Turkish courts are not truly independent.

Prosecutors and judges are appointed by a committee with a majority of government officials. In this situation, going against government wishes could lead to demotion or appointment to a remote post. There are some independent-minded prosecutors who have survived the system, like Aytac Tolay, who has openly denounced the anti-democratic laws he has had to implement in prosecuting journalists and writers. Exceptions like Tolay, which are found in all quarters of Turkey, are a testament to the stubborn persistence of democratic values despite all pressures to the contrary. The majority of prosecutors, however, are under the direct influence of the government.

Just before the European Union voted to grant Turkey favorable trade agreements—but not full membership in the Union—scores of trials against journalists ended with acquittal. Many Turks believed that there must have been an order from high up asking for acquittals while the EU considered Turkey's application. Soon after the Union approved the trade accord, however, the same journalists were convicted on similar charges.

The strengths and weaknesses of the Turkish press relative to the power of the government are evident in the case of *Evrensel* (Global), a moderate socialist daily. In an example of the kind of gross maltreatment of journalists that still occurs, albeit less than it used to, an *Evrensel* reporter, Metin Goktepe, was beaten to death by police while in detention in January 1996. Police tried to cover up the beating despite scores of witnesses. However, *Evrensel* and Goktepe's colleagues in the high-circulation mainstream media would not let the case be swept under the carpet. After constant bickering in the media for three months, the courts reluctantly brought the officers suspected of Goktepe's murder to trial.

But *Evrensel*'s insistence on the prosecution of the police officers responsible for its reporter's death cost the paper dearly. Before the Goktepe case, *Evrensel* had been acquitted in 10 trials. Days after a court announced its decision to try the officers, other courts started convicting *Evrensel* under Articles 6 and 7 (which forbid the publishing of statements and propaganda, respectively, from terrorist organizations), sentencing its editors to prison and ordering the paper shut down for short periods. After the prosecution of the police, conviction after conviction followed. Within a two-month period, the daily was ordered shut down a total of 95 days—which would practically force it out of business. The convictions are being appealed, and the appeals court's attitude will depend on the new government's view.

In its efforts to integrate with the West, Turkey has found a unique way to look democratic while still silencing the free press: doing it all under the cloak of law. When the Turkish government is attacked by its Western allies for putting pressure on its media, the defense is simple: We have no control over the judiciary; our country is based on laws, and our laws are no different than the ones you have.

True, banning the act of "inciting racism" sounds like a reasonable law. But Turkish courts, under heavy influence—to put it mildly—from the government, have used that law and many others to muzzle all unorthodox views, especially those that criticize the racist war against the Kurds. The mainstream media and even some alternative press have been "tamed" by this effective method. The loser, as usual, has been the public. On important issues, neither the Turks nor the Kurds are informed about what is happening within their own country.

The writer, a Turkish journalist based in Turkey, feared legal reprisal for this article and preferred to use a pseudonym.

Part IV

Civil Unrest

13

Algerian Journalists—
Casualties of a Dirty War

Taoufiq Derradji

In Algeria, a crazy slaughter has set the country on fire. No one can say exactly what the death toll is—50,000? 60,000?—but no one has been spared. Killings of civilians, including children, through terrorist bombings, torture and rape are part of everyday life. Powerless, grief-stricken, silent citizens watch their country sink into bloody turmoil.

Journalists are among this dirty war's casualties—59 of them as of August 1996. As the only witnesses of this underreported warfare, theirs is a highly perilous trade. They are caught between an oppressive government and murderous armed Islamic groups.

In Algeria, the life of the journalist has become an anonymous, fugitive existence. Your day begins with a journey to the newsroom—and if you take a taxi, as many journalists do, you change cabs during your trip to confuse anyone who may be following you. You exit the taxi far from the newsroom, so no one will know that you work at a newspaper or a broadcasting studio. You spend the day at your desk, avoiding public exposure. As the day ends, the pressure of your deadline fades into the anxiety of your trip home and one more circuitous taxi ride. Once you are home you stay indoors. Banks, shops and restaurants are dangerous places: You remember Saïd Mekbel, editor in chief of the daily *Le Matin,* shot down in an Algiers restaurant. Your entire existence is defined by your home, your newsroom and the taxi ride between them.

The fear of living under the threat of assassination seeps into your home life. Family members often tell journalists to get out of the profession. When I was working at the Algiers weekly *L'Observateur,* I was afraid to take my son to school, afraid to visit my wife in her office, and wary of the people around me on the street.

How did we get there? Why have hatred and violence taken hold of the regime and the fundamentalists? Why and how did journalists become hostages of the conflict?

It all began on Oct. 5, 1988. Young demonstrators, angered by a stagnant economy and a distant government, rose against the one-party regime of the FLN *(Front de Liberation Nationale)* that had dominated Algeria since it won independence from France in 1962. As they marched through the city, they destroyed all the symbols of the state. A bloody fight against the police followed, hundreds died, and Islamist critics of the government emerged as voices for popular anger. The FLN regime was eventually destabilized and could survive only by committing itself to democracy in 1989.

After 30 years of an austere political life, with a one-party system, a centralized economy and a state-dominated press, the used-up and discredited FLN regime tried to create a transition to democracy. Under the pressure of a fledgling journalistic movement, and willing to give the country instruments of political pluralism, the government opened the way for a free press in Algeria.

In 1987, there were only a dozen publications, six of them dailies. From 1989 to 1991, there were 103 newspapers and magazines, 16 of them dailies. The only television and radio station, however, remained under state control.

This political opening was short-lived. The first pluralistic legislative elections were canceled by the government in January 1992 when it became certain that the Islamists of the FIS *(Front Islamique de Salut,* or Islamic Salvation Front) would win. A state of emergency was proclaimed, and the Islamist press was forbidden. The FIS, robbed of its electoral victory, was dissolved and driven into an illegal underground existence. Thousands of Islamist critics of the regime were arrested and imprisoned in improvised detention camps.

Some Islamists, denied the right to express themselves in the open, turned to violence to accomplish their goals. The regime, its legitimacy contested, was determined to confront them and fight for its rights and privileges.

Journalists were caught between two fires. Islamists considered them traitors for having "approved" of the interruption of the electoral process. The government accused them of being allies of the Islamist terrorists because the media publicized their terrorist acts. Freedom of speech shrank as Algeria sank deeper into war. Even worse, journalists, as the last witnesses of the "democratic process," were condemned to be the victims of the tragedy unfolding before their eyes.

Confronted with the double threat of armed Islamists and an oppressive regime, journalists chose to save their own lives before addressing "freedom" of speech.

On the one hand, the terrorists promised "to slay with weapons those who fight with a pen." On the other hand, the regime attempted to domesticate those whom they perceived as being responsible for the strife shaking the country. Journalists faced "murder or the muzzle."

Long before terrorists actually killed a journalist, the practice of making death threats by mail or anonymous phone calls was frequent. Lists of journalists were posted in mosques or published in illegal leaflets. Preachers proclaimed *fatwas,* or edicts, urging their followers to hate and to murder.

In May 1993, the terrorists found their first victim, the writer-journalist Tahar Djaout. A month later, an anonymous letter to an Algiers editor in chief labeled Djaout "an extremist of the French-speaking world, a fierce enemy of the Koran, of Islam and of the national identity." Since then, fear has pervaded every newsroom.

Hunted down, journalists had to change their daily way of life. They progressively went underground; they were careful not to spend two nights in a row in the same place; they routinely changed their schedules and their routes to the office and back home; they avoided giving out their address and phone numbers. They got rid of their press cards. Despite those security measures, many journalists died in action, pen in hand, their last testimony being not ink on a newspaper but their own blood on the ground.

Terrorists did not spare newspaper buildings from attack. In February 1996, a bomb exploded in the Algiers *Maison de la Presse,* headquarters to almost all independent French- and Arabic-language publications founded in 1990 when the print press was granted more freedom. Many were killed.

Meanwhile, the government uses its political power to harass, threaten, arrest and arbitrarily imprison journalists. The regime seeks to domesticate a press that, in its opinion, has enjoyed too much of a freedom that led to bloody violence. Censorship, newspaper seizures and prohibitions of publishing and writing have swept away the ephemeral "freedom of speech" that each one of us experienced between 1989 and 1991.

Since 1992, restricting legislation and regulations have attacked the freedom of the press and have muzzled journalists:

El Watan, a French-language daily, was suspended for nine days in January 1993, for "prematurely" informing about the assassination of

five members of the army. Its publisher and four journalists were arrested and put under detention.

Al-Jazair al-Youm, an Arabic-language daily, was suspended in August 1993, for printing a fundamentalists' statement criticizing death
penalties pronounced by "special courts of justice."

For disclosing information about desertions from the army in March
1994, a journalist and the publisher of *L'événement* were arrested. They
were released two weeks later.

The publisher and a journalist for the French-language daily *Liberté*—
meaning "freedom"—were imprisoned on the charge of "repetitive
publishing of libelous information." The newspaper was suspended for
two weeks in December 1995.

Since June 1994, another state rule has demanded that journalists
rely on the national press agency as their "only source of information"
whenever the news has anything to do with security, such as executions, terrorist attacks, sabotage, fights involving the military or human
losses. On top of that, this agency is permitted to release only information it gets from the Ministry of Interior "communication unit."

The regime's communication policy aims at "preventing, fighting
against and winning over the enemy's spreading of rumors and propaganda." It also aims at "reducing the psychological impact on the population that the terrorist leaders hope for." A "specific terminology" was
set up by the people in power so that journalists do not "use unwit-
tingly a terminology that would be favorable to the adversary's ideology and propaganda." Again, this measure is one more attack on
journalists' independence, denying them any freedom of investigation
and analysis. It brings them back to the worst era of one-party rule,
when there was no free press.

The regime also created "reading committees." Since November
1994, professional censors have been responsible for preventing news
related to terrorism and its repression from being published. This brings
us back to the early years. Other practices condemn journalists and the
press to economic asphyxia: State subsidies and advertising, a state
monopoly, are granted to the press on a discriminatory basis. Cliques
and clans within the high echelons of the ruling party distribute funds
to their friends and allies in the press.

Journalists are, unwillingly, participants in the regime's institutional,
authoritarian information strategy. Not only are they prohibited from
releasing all the news, but the political powers incite them "to stress
the inhumane characteristics of the terrorists' barbaric practices: the

throat-cuttings, the assaults on ambulances, the killings and maimings of children, the assassinations of members of security services' parents...." Such a strategy keeps journalists in a climate of terror.

All murders committed by the Islamic groups are publicized. Murders committed by the security forces must be silenced. In fact, what journalists are being asked to do is to support the regime's action and fight against terrorists in the name of democracy. In light of all the restrictions on journalists, this reduces democracy to meaning "the fight against terrorism."

Since 1992, the regime, under the cover of the fight against terrorists, has remodeled the media system. Journalists who might be tempted to express understanding for moderate Islamists have seen their newspapers censured or suspended. Arabic-speaking journalists were the first victims of this strategy, but French-speaking journalists too cope daily with the regime's attacks and pressure. And those journalists working for television and radio, which are effectively controlled by the state, have been muzzled.

Journalists are pressured to have a complacent attitude toward the regime's action. Hard questions on human-rights violations or abuse by security forces are not to be asked. In a country where those in power speak anonymously as "well-informed sources," journalists are requested to justify what cannot be justified and give sense to the senseless. It is an unrewarding role.

Pressure can be formidable when one knows and has seen but cannot write. This disinformation, as mandated by the state, feeds terror.

The state's strategy relies on a repressive judicial system. Arrests, condemnations and detentions for questioning have become common practice, reinforcing the pressure that makes journalists comply. The political powers that be use compliant judges to tame journalists. By acting through judges, they run fewer risks of being identified with unpopular decisions.

Those strategies generate rumors. Rumors feed terror. Journalists' self-censorship induces unexpected effects. Islamic fundamentalists respond to all of this with more murders of journalists, which the press cannot conceal.

Despite their enormous burdens, journalists have no alternative but to preserve what is left of freedom. Their strength resides in acts of solidarity among newspapers. Each time a journalist is murdered, almost all newspapers go on a printing strike or leave one page blank in a sign of mourning. Each time a journalist gets arrested or imprisoned, the solidarity movement spreads: Journalists meet, write protest articles, sign a petition condemning the regime or go on strike.

Journalists refuse to be objective allies to the regime. They claim, with the expected sacrifices, their freedom to write and speak out. Knowing that the press is their only means of expression, journalists play the role of parliament. They have, for public opinion, a duty to perform. Public opinion is demanding. It does not tolerate servile journalists. It knows perfectly well that journalists take part in a tragedy, and it wants to know about it.

Many journalists have courageously kept writing, some of them using pseudonyms. Others, who could not take the situation any longer, have fled their country, lonely and bitter.

While Algerian journalists are in effect hostages, the regime exploits them politically and finds in them a reason for fighting against terrorism. When terrorists kill, the regime benefits from it. The more illegitimate the regime is, the more it needs journalists to justify its politics. And the journalists need, for their own survival, to negotiate with the regime. Financial and economic imperatives endanger the existence of a private press. The regime will keep threatening the press economically by raising printing costs and the prices of subscribing to the national press agency. This method has already succeeded.

Yet even if censorship and arrests continue, which is likely, the regime will not be able to suppress the independent press. The regime uses the presence of the independent press as an excuse to tout "democracy." And this, in a harsh economic situation, helps the state to obtain financial loans.

The journalism profession is becoming a barometer for democracy. Journalists are, and will remain, "lonely" professionals. But whatever hardship they have to go through, they will have enough moral resources to resist and set themselves free from both a criminal barbarism and authoritarianism.

Taoufiq Derradji, formerly a journalist in Algeria, lives in France.

14

In America, Justice for Some

Ana Arana

On the night of Sept. 22, 1990, as Vietnamese-American journalist Le Triet returned home from a party with his wife, Tuyet Thi Dangtran, two hit men waited in the dark. Triet's enemies had given the final order to kill the controversial columnist because of his critical stories on the fund-raising practices of a local paramilitary group.

The hit men were concealed in the Virginia night despite the floodlights that Triet had installed recently because of death threats. As he parked the car, one of the men quickly approached the driver's window and, before Triet could respond, fired several deadly shots. Triet's wife Tuyet attempted to escape, but the second gunman ran and killed her.

Triet's murder shocked the Vietnamese-American community. He was the fifth Vietnamese-American journalist slain in the United States since 1981 in a killing spree that spread through California, Texas and Virginia. And he was the second employee at the Virginia-based *Tien Phong* magazine murdered within 10 months. Like the Vietnamese-language newspapers where the other victims worked, Triet's magazine had taken a critical position against Vietnamese exile groups and their fund-raising techniques.

But the killings of Triet and other Vietnamese-American journalists were hardly unique. Over the last decade, 10 immigrant journalists have been murdered in the United States of America. In a country where it is widely assumed that reporters are safe from violence, their deaths are a reminder that the protections of the First Amendment are imperfectly applied, that mainstream reporters are generally much safer than their immigrant counterparts and that the tendency to put immigrant journalists in a separate category leaves them in dangerous isolation.

The Vietnamese, like most of the other immigrant journalists, were hit by violence because they, unlike reporters for mainstream press, remained participants and key players in their communities. In this respect, they practiced an engaged, combative style of journalism long ago abandoned by the mainstream American press.

Sometimes, because they are not aware of issues of fairness and stringent sourcing, immigrant journalists make mistakes that hurt people. This characteristic is more than matched, however, by their embrace of the United States' protection for a free press.

Their killers also embrace the United States but ignore the laws and customs of press freedom. They hold on to the Latin American, African and Asian traditions of lashing out at journalists who are too persistent and too daring, who challenge the powers that be.

In the 10 killings of immigrant journalists in the last decade, the U.S. law enforcement community and the media failed the victims. In most cases, quick response and sound investigations would have stopped the violence with the first murder. That lack of immediate response only gave the green light to further abuses.

Immigrants aside, in the United States no reporter works with the assumption that her life will be put in danger by a particular story. The last two journalists murdered because of their work were *Arizona Republic* reporter Don Bolles, killed in a 1976 mob hit, and Denver radio commentator Alan Berg, killed in a 1992 attack by white supremacists. After both murders, a firm response from the news media and from law enforcement left the indelible mark that reporters' lives were not fair game. Federal authorities investigated the mob and the white supremacists. After the Bolles murder, dozens of U.S. reporters descended on Arizona to finish the story Bolles left unfinished. (The effort gave birth to the association known as Investigative Reporters and Editors.) Both cases were solved within a relatively short time, although it took 17 years to finally nab the mastermind of Bolles' death.

The Bolles and Berg cases reminded Americans that the First Amendment works because U.S. citizens understand its importance. When people violate it, the courts and the authorities enforce it.

For immigrant journalists, however, the First Amendment offers no such protection: It is not accepted as a given right by all members of the immigrant communities, and U.S. authorities fail to enforce it there.

Out of 10 immigrant journalists killed in the last decade, only two cases have been solved. Besides the five Vietnamese Americans, three of the dead journalists were Haitian Americans, one was Chinese American and one was Cuban American. Four of the murders occurred in the last five years. The last murder was in 1993.

In most cases, the U.S. media and law enforcement agencies were initially interested in the murders. But as it became evident that considerable time and resources would be needed to solve them, the interest died out.

The Vietnamese Americans were killed between 1980 and 1990, a tumultuous decade in Vietnamese exile politics in the United States. As the communities swelled up with recent arrivals, competing groups of former young South Vietnamese officers attempted to organize a resistance movement against communist rule in Vietnam. The refugee population was hounded for support and donations. One group was supposed to have earned upwards of $200 million in donations. There were abuses, and the first ones to notice them were Vietnamese journalists many of whom had also joined the resistance groups.

A power struggle ensued between 1981 and 1990. The first victim was Lam Trong Duong, the only leftist sympathizer among the victims, who was killed in San Francisco in 1981. Nobody complained about this murder, since Duong was not a popular man among his countrymen.

But Duong's murder set the blueprint for the 1982 slaying of Nguyen Dam Phong, a staunch anti-communist publisher who was killed in Houston. In 1987, publisher Tap Van Pham was killed in Garden Grove, Calif. In Fairfax County, Va., the hit men got Nhan Trong Do in 1989 and Le Triet in 1990. They were killed after they criticized the fundraising tactics of the National Front for the Liberation of Vietnam: They charged that the money supposedly collected for a Thailand-based resistance army was instead filling the pockets of the group's leaders.

Several clues emerged that tied the murders together. A team of local, state and federal authorities took over the case and began an investigation that attempted to find a common killer. Within six months, however, the probe was off, with few leads.

Most of the difficulties faced by investigators were connected to problems of language and culture. Few of the investigating agencies, especially the FBI, had agents with either Vietnamese language skills or a feel for Vietnamese culture.

When Nguyen's paper ran exposés on the financial dealings of one exile group, it crushed the fund-raising efforts of a powerful sector of his community. And the five journalists killed had been integral players in the power-grab taking place among competing exile groups that wanted to organize the refugee community to support a resistance army to fight Hanoi's Communist government. All of the victims except for one were former members of the South Vietnamese military or intelligence community who had also worked as journalists in their country. Before getting killed, they had been members of one or another exile paramilitary group that supported the overthrow of the Vietnamese government.

While the five Vietnamese murders could have been prevented if authorities had better working knowledge of the Vietnamese community's inner conflicts, such knowledge is not a cure-all. In the case of three murdered Haitian immigrant journalists, however, authorities were aware of conflicts, but their investigations were crippled in part by a reluctance to take claims of persecution seriously.

Jean Claude Olivier and Fritz Dor were killed in 1991; Dona St. Plite in 1993. These immigrant Haitian journalists were all vocal supporters of President Jean-Bertrand Aristide. They were also well-known critics of the military junta that took power in a coup and ruled Haiti between 1991 and 1994.

The three, all broadcasters, voiced their opinions in weekly Creole-language news programs aired in Miami's Little Haiti. Their names appeared on death lists put together by supporters of the Haitian military in Miami.

St. Plite was killed during a mass commemorating the one-year anniversary of Fritz Dor's murder. The slayings were carried out by well-known members of Haitian-Bahamian gangs hired to kill the broadcasters. The killers used the same gun in two of the murders.

Investigators admit that the murders were contract hits, but they have never identified the persons who paid for them. Federal authorities never participated in the investigations because they argued that the killings had no interstate dimension that would mandate a federal response.

Several pieces of evidence tying the murders to Haiti and the Haitian military have never been fully explored, however. Why? Because the three broadcasters engaged in political activity and used the airwaves to broadcast their ideas. Also, federal authorities, whose attitude toward President Aristide ranged from lukewarm to hostile, were not inclined to believe claims of military persecution coming from his supporters. And the pro-Aristide Miami community did not have the clout to force federal authorities to reconsider the cases.

As the Haitian cases show, a new community, beset by violence, has a hard time attracting the interest of U.S. authorities. High-level investigative efforts that combine federal, state and local authorities are expensive. They must fit another agenda before they will benefit an immigrant community.

Indeed, of the 10 immigrant journalist murders, the only two solved involved either communities that were adept at demanding attention or had the benefit of a broader government agenda.

Henry Liu, a member of the media-savvy San Francisco Chinese-American community, was slain in 1984 by a hit team sent by the Taiwanese government, which had been angered by his critical press reports. The Liu case became a *cause célèbre* in the Bay Area's Asian-American community, which formed a special community committee to keep track of the investigation. Federal authorities were not let off the hook until the suspects were indicted and prosecuted. Prompt clarification of the murder was helped by the overall U.S. policy of strengthening relations with China. News that embarrasses Taiwan pleases Beijing and the prosecution of Taiwanese hit men could hardly damage America's standing in China.

Manuel de Dios Unanue was killed in 1992 in Queens, New York. A Cuban American and the outspoken former editor of *El Diario/La Prensa,* he had a reputation for writing tough stories about drugs and money-laundering. His killer was a hit man sent by leaders of the Colombian Cali Cartel. After a few initial mix-ups, the de Dios murder investigation was pushed forward by drug enforcement officials, who wanted an indictment against members of the Cali Cartel.

A complete task force was set up that eventually targeted and identified all the killers and middlemen. The de Dios murder was a complex case with several layers of participants, but it was solved because of a deep interest on the part of the law enforcement community. The U.S. Justice Department had even been preparing an indictment against one of the intellectual authors of the crime, José Santacruz Londoño, when he was killed recently in Cali by police.

The effective and quick response by the immigrant communities, law enforcement agencies and the Justice Department to these two murders sealed any possibilities that a similar crime could occur. Both Taiwan and the Cali Cartel learned that they could not attack journalists in the United States.

The lack of prosecution in the Vietnamese and Haitian murders, however, left permanent scars in both communities. Political terrorism has subsided in the Vietnamese-American community, but not for the best of reasons. There is no need to kill people because a simple warning does the trick for most Vietnamese journalists. The absence of justice in the five journalists' murders set a precedent that reverberates in the wave of common crime that has terrorized Vietnamese citizens in this country. U.S. authorities have a difficult time obtaining convictions on many criminal cases because Vietnamese-Americans, who have lost faith in the American justice system, are afraid to testify.

The FBI and the Justice Department reopened the Vietnamese investigations after an in-depth report on the murders by the Committee to Protect Journalists revealed a lack of proper police work. But in the last year, resources again have been assigned to other more high-profile cases.

Miami's Haitian community, divided along political lines even after democracy has been reinstalled in Haiti, cannot push for a comprehensive investigation. A Miami-based Haitian undercover investigator who followed the Miami murders, despondent over the lack of both progress in the cases and federal interest, said: "I know they go all the way to Haiti. I have names of people I would like to interview, but my department is not suited to follow these leads. And I don't know who to turn to for help."

The media also bear some of the blame for the lack of justice in the deaths of these immigrant journalists. Media interest has been intermittent and more focused on the headlines than in endorsing sound prosecution for the murders because, overall, the media cover ethnic communities only when they are the scene of violent or sensational stories. Reporters covered the murders but turned away from covering the vital but tedious story of the subsequent investigations.

Vicky de Dios, who has continued to put pressure to get the last defendant tried and convicted for her husband's murder, agrees that even in his case the media were interested only when it was a front-page story. Final sentencing for three of the six original defendants is pending. Because some of them cooperated with authorities, lower sentences are expected. But Vicky De Dios feels that even in those cases the sentences should not be reduced because that would send the wrong message to the killers, "but I can't get anybody in the media to stay on top of the story," she says. "I know the power of the media. If it wasn't for their interest, the case would not have gone forward in the first place. But there is lack of follow through."

The 10 murdered immigrant journalists came to the United States to escape political strife in Vietnam, Haiti and Latin America. Once here, they did not take extraordinary safety precautions or censor their writing—things they might have done if they had remained in their home countries. After all, they were in the United States. They believed that here they were free to express their opinions about internal debates in their communities. They believed in freedom of the press.

Their deaths were a threat to journalists. And when Americans failed to bring their killers to justice, they let down their own best traditions of press freedom and equal justice. "When you don't solve these cases," says Doug Zwemke, a longtime California investigator who followed the Vietnamese murders, "you're sending a message that these people are not protected by the laws of the United States."

Ana Arana, a free-lance investigative journalist, previously ran the Americas program for the Committee to Protect Journalists, where she initially investigated these cases.

Part V

Organized Crime

15

Blood and Fear in Italy

Candida Curzi

The first to die, in the memory of journalists of my generation—that is, those old enough to have worked 20 years in a newsroom and young enough to still be in front of the computer—was Mauro De Mauro.

It was September 1970. De Mauro, editor of the small, local Palermo paper *L'Ora,* was working for one of the most famous Italian directors, Francesco Rosi, to reconstruct the last hours spent in Sicily of Enrico Mattei, the director of the Ente Nazionale Idrocarburi (National Hydrocarbon Authority), who had died in an air accident. De Mauro was kidnapped and never heard from again. Colleagues, friends and investigators all understood immediately: It was a case of *lupara bianca.*

Lupara bianca roughly translates as *sawed-off shotgun.* But for Italians it carries an extra meaning: a victim of the *lupara bianca* is one of the hundreds of persons in Sicily kidnapped and killed by the Mafia, whether for publicizing Mafia crimes or as punishment for some perceived affront to one of the "families," whose body is never recovered.

De Mauro's case was typical. Without a body, without anyone willing to talk about it, nothing could be proven. Twenty-five years later, however, Tommaso Buscetta, a Mafioso who turned states' evidence, interviewed in a book by sociologist Pino Arlacchi, revealed: "We killed De Mauro as a favor to the American *Cosa Nostra,"* which, in turn, was probably doing a favor for the large petroleum companies whose political interests were linked to the ENI, Mattei's agency. Prosecutors are taking Buscetta's accusations seriously. They have reopened investigations and exhumed the bodies of the crash victims to search for new forensic evidence of an explosion. They are also re-examining tests done on the wreckage of the airplane at the time of Mattei's death.

The latest target was Chiara Beria D'Argentine. It happened on May 24 of 1996: Her weekend home in Tuscany, which was fortunately empty, was blown up by a concealed bomb.

On the same day, *L'Espresso,* the popular Italian newsweekly of which Beria is deputy editor, came out with a cover story under her byline. It was dedicated to Ilda Boccasini, the magistrate who arrested the killers of Giovanni Falcone, a prominent magistrate who was investigating the Mafia. To some reporters and police, the bombing of Beria D'Argentine's house on the day she published a story dedicated to an opponent of the Mafia was too rich in symbolism to be an accident. Investigations of the episode continue, but in the absence of any informers it is difficult to attribute responsibility to the Mafia.

Between the De Mauro and Beria D'Argentine incidents, five journalists died:

Mino Pecorelli, director of a small news agency linked to the journal OP *(Osservatore Politica),* a publication reputed to have ties to the Italian Secret Service, was killed in Rome in March 1979 while investigating links between the Mafia, politics and business. According to the indictment of his killers and those who hired them, they were working for the *Cosa Nostra* to "do a favor for Sen. Andreotti." Sen. Giulio Andreotti, a leader of a faction of the Christian Democrats, went on to become prime minister.

Mario Francese, editor of the *Giornale di Sicilia* and a specialist in the Mafia, was killed in Palermo on Jan. 26, 1979.

Giuseppe Fava, founder and director of the anti-Mafia Catania periodical *I Siciliani,* was killed in January 1984. Fava, a journalist who specialized in the Mafia, was also active in the political fight against the Mafia and had organized conferences and demonstrations against it.

Giancarlo Siani, writer for the Naples daily *Il Mattino,* was slain in 1985 in Naples He was "killed," says the report of an anti-Mafia investigation committee, "because he decided to investigate collusion in the assignation of lands in Torre Annunziata between the then-mayor Domenico Bertone and the Gionta Mafia clan."

Giuseppe Alfano, schoolteacher and writer for the *Giornale di Sicilia,* was killed in Barcellona Pezzo di Gatto, near Gela, on Jan. 8, 1993, a town with a strong Mafia presence.

In April 1993, in Rome, a car bomb missed its target, the popular Italian talk show host, Maurizio Costanzo, by a matter of seconds but destroyed several buildings and a school. Miraculously, there was only one casualty.

In the last quarter century, there have been many bombs, whether placed in homes, cars, letters or even telephones. There have also been macabre warnings: mutilated animals left on doors or crosses drawn with chalk in the shape of a body, like the outlines police make at a murder scene. At first, they were meant for journalists who work on the front lines of Mafia coverage in the "region at risk"—southern Italy. Now, they are also left for the editors, anchormen and reporters who live in Rome or Milan.

It is a record of blood and fear that is small in comparison with the one suffered by magistrates and investigators killed by the dozens in Sicily and Calabria. And it is a price less horrible than that paid by the common victims: peasants killed by mistake or women and children of the "families" involved in the clan wars of the 1980s fought in Sicily and Calabria. Altogether, in the Mafia wars of the previous decade, more than 1,000 in southern Italy were dead or missing because of the *lupara bianca*. The investigators, and former Mafiosi who have come forward, tell of how the people thought to be missing were strangled, of how their bodies were burned in acid or buried in one of the since-discovered "Mafia cemeteries" or burned on a grill normally used to cook lamb or goat.

Only when the informers began to tell their stories, only after the anti-Mafia magistrate Falcone and his colleague Paolo Borsellino were killed in the summer of 1992, only after the horrible stories of their deaths received front-page coverage—only then did the vendetta and intimidation reach the highest levels of Italian journalism.

Before, in the 1970s, '80s, and early '90s, only local reporters told how Salvatore "Toto" Riina and his men controlled access to governmental power in Palermo, how the men of the *Camorra* in Naples and of the *'ndrangheta* in Calabria conquered the black market as well as the allocation of public lands and how this control was eventually defended by Kalashnikovs or car bombs. Then, only the provincial or free-lance journalists were targets of Mafia bullets or of death threats. Journalists such as De Mauro, Alfano, Fava, Siani and Francese were fine reporters, but they were not famous.

It was not so in the reporting of terrorism in the 1970s and '80s. Only the most noted reporters and commentators of the national news organizations were sent to cover the Red Brigades or the armed bands of neofascists. In 1977 alone, bullets wounded the directors of *Secolo XIX,* of *Il Giornale* and of the national television news program "Tg1" and killed the deputy editor of *La Stampa.* Three years later, a reporter for *La Repubblica* was wounded and one from *Corriere della Sera* was killed.

But from the start, the press and people in public life recognized the threat of terrorism. In 1979, Parliament approved measures making terrorists' sentences more severe, preparing more maximum security prisons and providing more instruments to the police in order to improve the investigation and prosecution of terrorism.

Until recently the Mafia did not receive this kind of attention. The Christian Democrats, the political party that dominated Italy until recently, used the Mafia to maintain power and were reluctant to direct attention to organized crime. Furthermore, the Mafia is an ancient phenomenon, and Italian public opinion had not caught up to the fact that the Mafia was no longer the local racketeers of the 1950s. During the 1970s, organized crime moved out of its traditional strongholds like western Sicily and conquered the rest of Sicily, Calabria and Campania. The Mafia expanded its extortion racket and enriched itself through the sale of drugs. It infiltrated local administrative offices, going as far as the police precincts and the judicial chambers. It crossed into the new markets of northern Italy.

While all of this happened, the Mafia was not written about for more than a few days at a time. A magistrate or a policeman would be killed, the government would discuss it and appoint a special investigator, only to leave him without power after the emotion of the moment passed.

News coverage died because investigations never went forward. It was difficult for journalists to sustain their reporting because the guilty parties were never discovered. Murders remained unsolved. Only since informers have come forward in the wake of Falcone's death have guilty parties been uncovered, spawning more coverage.

It took time for Italians to recognize the danger that the Mafia posed to democracy. At the end of 1989, Italy's chief of police, Prefect Vincenzo Parisi, delivered a speech at a high school. He defined the Mafia as an enemy of the Italian state, a threat to Italian democracy that practically had the force of a hostile power. Parisi denounced the enormous sway that the *Cosa Nostra* had seized. But it would take three years and terrible events for Italians, especially Italian journalists, to address the implications of Parisi's charge.

Judge Falcone, brought from Palermo to Rome to direct the division of Penal Affairs for the Ministry of Justice, mapped a new judicial geography with new guidelines for the prosecution of the Mafia. But it took his assassination in May 1992, followed by the killing of his colleague Borsellino in July 1992, to make the project a reality and give Italy an investigative, penal and judicial system that could effectively compete with organized crime. The media, too, reacted to the brutal impact of the events of 1992. Italian news organizations began to cover the Mafia on a regular basis and assigned their best reporters and news analysts to cover organized crime.

The Mafia itself contributed to the conditions that led to increased public attention when it turned to "Mafia terrorism," a term coined by Mafia investigator Gianni De Gennaro while smoke rose from the crater left by a car bomb in Florence in the spring of 1993. Five deaths were reported, including two children, the residents of houses that had faced that street; there was also heavy damage to the Uffizi museum. It was one of the first Mafia attacks intended not to eliminate an "enemy," but rather to create panic, to cause divisions in the government and to try to force changes in the laws on government informers and those that mandated tough sentences for Mafia bosses. De Gennaro's intuition was later confirmed by investigations and new informers— former Mafia men who "repented" and came forward in order to receive reduced sentences. They confirmed that the strategy, along with the idea of attacking art institutions, had been decided upon by Mafia boss Riina. Riina wanted to make political opinion surge against the anti-Mafia movement and push the government to cancel anti-Mafia laws and provisions. In short, it was an effort at political blackmail. Riina developed the plan in association with a right-wing terrorist whose comrades had attempted something similar in the 1970s.

In the fall of '92, before these attacks began, a study prepared by sociologists predicted such violence and provided a way of understanding these acts. The scholars argued that the Sicilian Mafia was "in the midst of a communications revolution." Instead of intimidating individuals they would now try to intimidate the entire nation. Their apparent goal: the preservation of their power and territorial control as well as a demonstration of its defiance of the state. The Mafia, the scholars said, went "from internal codes to public crimes of spectacle."

The sociologists proposed that members of the press take into account their findings and work on the basis of their previous experiences with terrorism. They encouraged journalists to avoid "any effect of legitimation," and to emphasize that in dealing with the Mafia one is always dealing with a criminal phenomenon, with an organization of delinquents seeking profit through crime. Journalists covered the release of the sociologists' report, but the coverage ended there. A year later, however, they saw that it provided an important analysis of events such as the killings of Falcone and Borsellino.

Today, four years after this analysis, four years after "crimes of spectacle" bathed Palermo, Rome, Florence and Milan in blood, there is another risk: that the television cameras will turn away, that the best journalists will turn again to other subjects, that the public will again forget. Journalists have short attention spans, and newspapers that print the same kind of story day in and day out sell fewer copies.

It is impossible to provide an armed escort for every journalist. The only way to make reporters safe is to eliminate the Mafia threat. And that will happen only through mobilized citizens and a mobilized judiciary.

Even today, when the Mafia uses the most modern communications technologies, one is reminded of the old Sicilian proverb "Piegati giunco che passa la piena," or "The reed that is bent has survived the storm."

Candida Curzi is a 20-year veteran at the Italian news service ANSA, where she has worked as a reporter and editor on national news, justice and security problems, terrorism and the Mafia. This essay was translated by Jeffrey Durland.

16

Veronica Guerin, In Life and Death

Compiled by Jennifer Kelley

Irish Reporter Veronica Guerin dedicated the last years of her too-short life to exposing the "violence, money and evil" of the Irish under-world. Someday her country and her colleagues will learn if they are worthy of her example.

Guerin, an acclaimed investigative reporter at the *Sunday Independent,* was murdered by two unidentified gunmen on the outskirts of Dublin on June 26, 1996. Her slaying was widely believed to be a contract killing, carried out by the Irish mob.

It was hardly the first act of violence against the married mother of a small boy, a latecomer to journalism who had also worked in accounting, politics and public relations. In October 1994 shots were fired at her home after she wrote about an Irish gangster—but no arrests were made. In January 1995, after she published a profile of the suspected mastermind of the biggest robbery in Irish history, a masked gunman broke into her home and shot her in the thigh—and no arrests were made. In September of 1995, an Irish businessman whom she sought to interview slammed her head into a car and threatened to kill her if she wrote about him and his family.

Through it all, she persevered. Guerin's reporting probed the web of drugs and violence in a society whose legal system seems inadequate to confront the threat of rising crime.

Until recently, people in Ireland could tell themselves, plausibly, that they lived in a country free from fear of criminals. Now they cannot. Guerin's reporting, and her death, are the proof.

In life, she was noted for being brave yet buoyant, passionate yet utterly factual. The best way to dredge some meaning from her death will be for journalists, police and government officials—for the Irish people—to stand up, as she did, for the protection of journalists and against the depredation of organized crime.

In Life—Standing Up for Reporters

by Veronica Guerin

Excerpted from her acceptance speech at the Committee to Protect Journalists' International Press Freedom Awards, December 1995.

It is very unusual to hear that an Irish reporter has been shot or intimidated. Unfortunately, because of the ever-rising crime problems in Ireland, a number of reporters, not just myself, have been subjected to death threats and to intimidation on a daily basis. So, for my colleagues in other newspapers and in the broadcast media, I'm grateful that the CPJ have decided to honor an Irish and European journalist.

Unfortunately, in Ireland, journalists have to face the threat of possible imprisonment, and I welcome this opportunity to highlight the appalling case of a colleague of mine who works in the *Irish Independent*. She is facing a possible jail sentence [for alleged breach of the Official Secrets Act] because she published a document which was widely circulated within the police force in Ireland about the suspects of a bank robbery...

We write under ridiculously restrictive laws in Ireland. It's a wonderful country, great place to visit, but, unfortunately for journalists, the most difficult thing we have to work within are our restrictive libel laws. It's difficult for publishers because they are the people who have to pay massive amounts of money on a daily basis in courts.

These are the issues that I feel that I have to highlight here. It's not the fact that journalists may be shot, but the legitimate restrictions that we work within....

In Death—Brave and Brilliant, With a Sense of Mischief

by Alan Byrne, editor, The Racing Post, London

Excerpted from his speech at the opening of The Freedom Forum European Center in London, June 27, 1996.

I still can't believe that I am never going to get another call from Veronica, that she won't be on the phone telling me about the stories she was working on, filling me in on the latest newspaper gossip from Dublin, and telling me how brilliant Manchester United are and how useless my team are.

Veronica was always on the phone.

Meet her for coffee and she would have not one but two mobile phones going off in stereo.

She used to buy all the papers after dropping her son, Cathal, at school in the morning. She would head for the same coffee shop every day and devour the papers, cigarettes and coffee all at once, pausing only to answer those phones.

She would talk for a while and then say, "Do you know who that was?" before outlining some often improbable tale. I say improbable. From any of the rest of us, they would have been improbable tales. But Veronica was different. She was a brilliant reporter. And when she came up with stories, no matter how remarkable they sounded, they generally proved to be correct.

She had extraordinary contacts. I have never met anybody who was so good with people. She was an open, warm person and she had an incredible talent for getting people to talk.

Every reporter in town would be chasing someone who would be easily evading the pack. But not Veronica. She would drive out to the person's house, wait for them to return and then try to persuade them to talk. Usually, she succeeded.

She had a way with people.

Sometimes, though, that was a problem.

Such as when four of us went to America for the World Cup in the summer of 1994. It was impossible to go to or from any of the grounds at any speed. You'd be walking toward the stadium, and Veronica would see somebody she recognized. Time and again we'd stop while Veronica exchanged greetings and information.

"That was the Taoiseach's daughter," she'd say. "That fellow is the accountant for one of the biggest criminals in Dublin, you know."

Whatever the story, she knew somebody who knew somebody who could tell her about it. "I'll make a call," she'd say, and that would be that. And once on to a story, she was so meticulous and so determined. She just wouldn't give up.

Others would avoid making difficult calls, say that the story just wasn't working, give up and head home. Not Veronica. She would keep going until she had the story—whatever the personal risks and dangers.

When she started writing about crime, she developed an extraordinary range of police and criminal contacts. And when she was shot in the leg in January of last year, some of those criminals got in touch to sympathize with her. Veronica, though, just wanted to find out who had ordered her to be shot. And when she found out, she went, on crutches, to see the person to let them know she wasn't scared.

I remember her telling me that her legs were shaking as she confronted the individual. But she wouldn't let him see it. She wouldn't be beaten.

That was typical of her.

It was typical of Veronica too that when she was shot she hated all the fuss. I was contacted at the time by one of the Irish papers and was quoted the next day as saying what a great reporter she was. By 10 o'clock, she was on the phone from her hospital bed. "I see you're still talking rubbish!" she said. After that, I remember saying to her that she didn't have to take the risks anymore. But she would have none of it. She became more and more determined. Her stories got better and better. She pioneered a new style of journalism in Ireland.

Two weeks ago she was on the phone, very excited, saying that her paper was going to name the three biggest heroin dealers in Dublin. Lacking her bravery, I urged her to be careful, said how dangerous it sounded. But her response was simple: "Somebody's got to do it...."

She cared about her work, was proud of her profession and wanted the drug barons to be made accountable for their actions.

I will remember her as a supremely dedicated and talented reporter. I will remember Saturday afternoons when, as news editor of the *Sunday Tribune,* I would watch the door of the newsroom or wait for the phone to ring, hoping against hope that she could rescue my failure to produce a decent story. Usually, she did.

I will remember her screaming obscenities at referees, all those phone calls and I will remember her devotion to her family, to her husband, Graham, and her son, Cathal. And her devotion to Manchester United. And to Eric Cantona, the team's French star.

When we had a drink after watching Ireland play Croatia three weeks ago, she told me of the trouble her devotion to the Frenchman had caused her. She had taken Cathal, who is seven, to be interviewed by the headmaster of his new school. Cathal was asked what sports he was interested in. Football, he said. And who is your favorite team? Manchester United. And your favorite player? Eric Cantona—my mom wants to make love to him.

Veronica liked that. She loved to laugh. She had a great sense of mischief and she never took herself seriously. When I congratulated her on the Committee to Protect Journalists award last year, she was utterly dismissive.

But it was a great achievement. And she achieved remarkable things in a tragically short journalistic career. The tragedy is that while she got close enough to the workings of the major criminals in Dublin to put her own life at risk, the authorities seem incapable of getting as close or of doing anything about it.

Veronica would be amused and horrified in equal measure if she knew that so many people were gathered here this evening paying tribute to her. She would say she wasn't worthy of the fuss. But she was.

She was a brave and brilliant reporter.

Part VI

Portfolio

17

Dangerous Exposures

Susan D. Moeller

> *"If your pictures are no good, you aren't close enough."*
> —Robert Capa, photographer

Among the thousands of images that confront us every day, the ones we recall are the striking ones, the radical ones, the ones both aesthetically and emotionally commanding. They are often the very photographs for which journalists risk their lives and their hearts.

Photographs aren't like prose. You can write a story from a desk back in the newsroom. But you have to be on the spot to take the picture. In World War II, during the drive across Europe, print correspondents frequently sprinted to just inside the city-limits sign of a town under attack to qualify for the prized dateline: "in Cherbourg" or "in Cologne." But photographers had to be on top of the action to get their pictures. And, of course, if photographers are close enough to shoot their pictures, they are more than close enough to get shot. Too many have. Over two-thirds of those journalists killed during the Vietnam War, for example, were photographers or cameramen.

Since the invention of cameras and film fast enough to capture action in the late 19th century, photographers have had to take their chances on the front lines of war and civil disturbances. And as technology improved and close-ups of action became possible, photographers increasingly took chances.

Western photographers first consistently took risks to capture war on film during the Spanish Civil War in the 1930s. The new and ubiquitous 35mm cameras made it possible to go anywhere and take photos of anything, and the war itself, which put civilians and entire cities under attack, necessitated intrepid photographic effort.

By the Second World War, photographers had become old hands in combat. In one of the last Pacific landings, the comparatively green troops followed the photographers because the photographers were the veterans. The journalists told the soldiers to move away and to spread out. That was a better tactic and also a better picture. But the troops stuck close. "It didn't do our films any good," said one photographer, "but it sure was flattering."

It has always been difficult to capture the experience of war, death and destruction on film. Photographers can try to figure out where the stories are, they can calculate the risks of a certain shot, but often it comes down to luck. They can be there and snap the picture at the precise moment when it all comes together in one beautifully composed shot, or they can wait all day in the thick of the fighting and nothing remotely photogenic comes along. They can run out of film at precisely the wrong instant or their camera can jam. Or the censors can appropriate their film or deny them access to where they need to be. Savvy censors and thugs the world over have learned that a picture is more dangerous than the verbal telling of an event—and that when opportunities to take pictures are denied, international news interest wanes.

Photographers have routinely put themselves in the path of fighting, but the ante has been repeatedly ratcheted higher. In the world wars, in Korea and even in Vietnam, journalists were generally accorded non-combatant status by both sides in the fighting. But since the war in Lebanon, war has become more Hobbesian, nastier and more brutish, and journalists have lost their neutral status. It takes a new kind of courage for photographers to venture out into a constantly shifting scenario. No telephoto lens is long enough to provide safety to a photographer when the rules of engagement have changed so much that even journalists have become targets.

Most photographers used to taking pictures in dangerous situations learn how to calculate—and minimize—the risks. They learn to travel in groups, to get passes from all sides—and then to stash them in different pockets.

Some photographers seek out risks because they love the urgency, the meaning it gives their lives and the edge it gives to their work. They get high on the danger—and are sickened by their addiction. Capa would curse a quiet day without battle because it meant no pictures, and then curse himself for being hungry for photographic carnage.

Sometimes photographers are tempted into believing that their camera is a kind of magic talisman. They think they can afford to get close to the action because their cameras offer them a strange immunity. The camera is a shield; as long as they peer through the lens, they are on the outside looking in—they cannot get hurt. Margaret Bourke-White said about photographing Buchenwald: "I kept telling myself that I would believe the indescribably horrible sight in the courtyard before me only when I had a chance to look at my own photographs. Using the camera was almost a relief; it interposed a slight barrier between myself and the white horror in front of me."

In 1980, Salvadoran army troops murdered three American nuns and one lay missionary. The press was present when their bodies were exhumed. One of the photographs taken that day shows the slain women's bodies being dragged from their shallow grave as four photographers capture the scene on film. Through these photographers, we became witnesses. Their images prompted many in the U.S. to action. Others just turned the page—sadder, wiser, but relatively unscathed.

But photographers cannot turn the page on what they see. How, then, do they cope when confronted with the "white horror" when the death and destruction are overwhelming, and individual effort seems futile? How does a photographer weigh the responsibility to bear witness against the responsibility to be involved? Can you help one victim and not all the others?

Getting "Capa" close means being close enough to help those who are being photographed. A moral dilemma ensues of whether to be an observer or a participant. The dilemma as typically construed opposes presumably "callous" detachment with "compassionate" intervention, the presumption being that direct aid to one victim is preferable to the more remote yet wider effect of a published photograph.

Kevin Carter, a white South African photojournalist who risked his life to photograph the evils of apartheid and the ravages of black factional violence, confronted that dilemma when he went to the Sudan. There, he snapped the iconographic image of a starving little girl crawling towards a UN feeding station while a black hooded vulture waited patiently behind her.

He never knew whether she had made it to the feeding station; in the immediate vicinity people were dying at the rate of 20 an hour. His job was to get the story out. He did and won the Pulitzer Prize for his effort. Two months after he accepted the award in New York he committed suicide. He told a friend, "I'm really, really sorry I didn't pick the child up."

Like Carter, the most engaged and humane photographers reach a point when the totality of what they have seen becomes unbearable. Reporters can write through their darkest experiences as a catharsis, but photographers, who rarely even process their own film, can only internalize what they witness. As writer Michael Herr said of one Vietnam War photographer: "I'll never forget what he looked like, that frontline face. He never got anything on film that he didn't get on himself...."

Photographers deserve both greater support and greater recognition for the effort it takes to report on global crises. The many free-lancers and stringers who make up such a large part of this workforce need such basics as health care and survivor benefits. In the United States there has been a great deal of attention given to the stress suffered by the military veterans of foreign wars—especially Vietnam—but little given to the journalist veterans.

Photographers often have to put themselves in peril to bring their photographs home. The risks they run are more than physical and last for more than a moment of danger, but their pictures can make an enduring difference in how we see the world. Without their consistent courage under fire, under threat, under duress, we at home would know too little about the most troubled spots in the world—and that too little would usually be just what the perpetrators of violence and aggression want us to know.

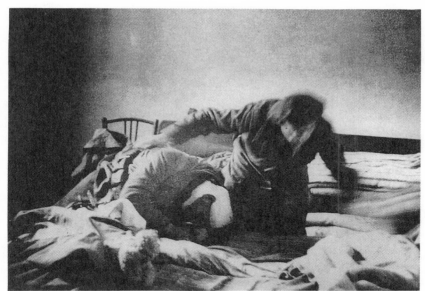

Robert Capa, Life. *Madrid, Spain, 1936.*   © Robert Capa/Magnum Photos

During the Spanish Civil War, at the very moment of a bomb's impact, Capa photographed wounded defenders of Madrid.

Boris Kudoyarov, From the Russian War

Boris Kudoyarov, Komsomolskaya Pravda. *Leningrad, USSR, World War II.*

Factory workers run from an exploding bomb in Nievsky Prospekt. Kudoyarov, a founder of Soviet photojournalism, hardly left the city during its 900-day siege.

Charles Moore. Birmingham, Ala., May 1963. © Charles Moore/Black Star

Demonstrators are pummeled by high-pressure hoses capable of stripping the bark off trees. As a civil rights-era photographer, Moore favored 33mm and 28mm lenses that put him close to the action.

Anonymous, UPI. Sanada, Iran, August 1979. UPI/Corbis-Bettmann

The Ayatollah Khomeini government ordered the execution of these nine Kurdish rebels and two former police officers of the deposed Shah in an attempt to show the futility of guerrilla fighting. The photograph was awarded the Pulitzer Prize anonymously to protect the photographer.

Andree Kaiser, free-lance photographer. Newsday. *Manjaca, Bosnia-Herzegovina, July 1992.*

During a tour of a Serbian army-run prisoner-of-war camp, guards surrounded Kaiser to ensure he only took authorized photos. Kaiser feigned boredom, passed out cigarettes to the guards and, when no one was looking, snapped three frames of the prisoners' heads being shaved several hundred yards away.

Kevin Carter, free-lance photographer. New York Times. *Ayod, Sudan, March 1993.*

After Carter took his photographs, he chased the bird away and watched as the little girl resumed her struggle. A little more than a year later he committed suicide.

Ron Haviv. Time. *Moscow, Russia, October 1993.*   © Haviv/Saba

To shoot this photograph, Haviv stood in mob of Communists, neo-Nazis and hooligans who faced a cordon or riot police surrounding the White House of President Boris Yeltsin.

John F. Trow's Alton Trials (1838). Library of Congress

In the 19th century, when mob attacks on journalists were common, abolitionist Elijah Lovejoy died defending his press.

Part VII

Solutions

18

Lessons from American History

John Nerone

As war loomed between a newly independent nation and its old colonial master, a newspaper editor called the imminent hostilities "unnecessary" and "expedient." A crowd answered him by demolishing his office. Relishing the thought of armed conflict, the editor fortified a house, set up shop and resumed publication. A crowd gathered and shots were fired. Troops quelled the violence and took the defenders of the newspaper to jail for safekeeping—whereupon the crowd destroyed the house and eventually turned on the jail, where they mercilessly beat the defenders who were unable to escape.

Tajikistan in 1996? No, Baltimore, Md., in 1812. The newspaper in question, the *Federal-Republican,* opposed the newly declared War of 1812 between Britain and America.

A nation's past can be like a foreign country, and it's often hard to see the connection between it and the present. The history of violence against the press in the United States is a case in point. We can't imagine today's *Baltimore Sun* being torn down by a mob for opposing a war.

The irony, however, is that the United States has a teeming tradition of violence against the press. You could write a book about it. (I did.)

But this violence was aimed at a press that was much different from today's. It was a press that understood itself and was understood as an active political instrument, whether as the committed advocate of a position or as the voice and face of a community. It behaved in ways that don't sit well with today's notions of responsible journalism, and it was held to standards that don't sit well with today's notions of press freedom.

Violence against journalists in the United States declined dramatically when journalism professionalized in the early 20th century. In part this came about because of broad social and cultural forces: the creation of a bureaucratized polity, for instance, and the appearance among lawyers and academics of a civil liberties elite. In large part it came about because of choices that journalists and publishers made. They decided to leave partisanship behind and define themselves as expert information gatherers and providers. This move gained them a measure of prestige, and with it security, but it also lost them a long tradition of engagement with the volatile issues of their time.

At the end of the 20th century, mainstream American journalists are far less likely to be the target of violence than their predecessors. True, immigrant journalists in the United States who cover volatile stories in the ethnic press are still the targets of killers. But that is because they practice the engaged, combative kind of journalism that once got mainstream American journalists into trouble. And most of the attacks on immigrant journalists spring from conflicts within their communities.

U.S. journalists remember Don Bolles, the *Arizona Republic* reporter blown up by a car bomb while investigating organized crime in the 1970s, as a good, aggressive and fearless reporter. Yet considering the ideology of U.S. reporting—the watchdog tradition, the adversarial stance, the call to be the advocate of the powerless—the surprising thing is that there haven't been more cases of this nature. If U.S. journalists do routinely get in the face of the powerful and dangerous, you would expect them to get blown up as often as journalists elsewhere. Instead, the only really common form of violence against U.S. journalists today is celebrities punching out photographers. The people that journalists fear are crazies and muggers, not the corrupt powerful that they aim to expose.

We assume that journalism is always and everywhere the same—reporters and editors getting the news. In fact, the U.S. has had several distinct press systems and many different kinds of journalism within them. Our relatively stable news media industry was preceded by a wildly competitive one—in 1930, New York City had about two dozen general-interest English language dailies (not counting Brooklyn and the Bronx) and even more foreign-language dailies. This highly commercial press was itself preceded by a vigorously partisan press. And sitting outside those dominant modes of journalism were other papers—reform papers, minority papers, religious papers, labor papers. These earlier journalisms were more likely to see violence, probably because they were more easily cast as illegitimate and so not deserving of protection.

The notion of broad protection for free expression is really rather recent. Americans, and American journalists, tend to assume that freedom of the press was enshrined in the U.S. at the time of the Revolution. The ratification (and the numbering) of the First Amendment confirms this assumption. At the time of the drafting of the Constitution, a broad range of people agreed that freedom of the press was a good thing, but they didn't necessarily mean freedom as we understand it. Freedom was understood as a middle ground between tyranny (no freedom) and licentiousness (too much freedom). And it was very easy to hurl a charge of licentiousness.

The history of the Revolutionary movement illustrates this point. Though they used the term freedom of the press with relish, the Revolutionaries were not in love with the idea of unrestricted political debate. Patriots argued strongly for their own freedom to publish, but they put their opponents in a different category—freedom of the press was for freedom fighters only. The Revolution was deadly serious, and to succeed the Revolutionaries needed to present themselves as the representatives of a unanimous public that agreed on the legitimacy of the movement and its novel political institutions.

The Revolutionaries did not rely on words alone; they also used propaganda of the deed. Patriotic enforcers hounded dissidents, and went to great lengths to make them seem corrupt, conspiratorial, and outside the community. Their targets, especially those who were tarred and feathered, thought of them as terrorists.

A few of these targets were printers, most notoriously James Rivington. Rivington had been a successful New York printer and bookseller, though always resented by some for his airs. As the Revolutionary crisis approached, his print shop and his newspaper, the Gazetteer, became obnoxious to Patriots because they were the only outlets for pamphleteers loyal to the Crown.

While Rivington claimed to be impartial, and argued that printing both sides of a controversy was a printer's duty, to Patriots it seemed that giving voice to Loyalists was not impartial at all. The very existence of a debate among colonials on the legitimacy of the Continental Congress, for instance, would be taken to mean that the Congress was not legitimate.

New York's Patriot leaders pushed Rivington to reject Loyalist pamphleteers, but their pressure did not satisfy the more radical elements of the Revolutionary movement. In the wake of the news of the battles at Lexington and Concord, a captain of privateers named Isaac Sears led a troop of volunteer, cavalry from Connecticut into New York City to attack Rivington's shop.

This was an acid test for faith in open political debate. The Patriot leadership failed. While they were upset with Sears for mobbing Rivington, it wasn't because he'd attacked the press—it was because he'd launched his attack from Connecticut, offending the Patriot leadership of New York and risking the coalition that directed the Revolutionary movement.

The founding generation wasn't particular about freedom of the press. It was not a key issue leading up to the Revolution, probably because the British had never really been able to hamper colonial printing. Instead, the crucial grievances against the British involved property, taxation and representation.

So the Revolution did not enshrine the notion of a free marketplace of ideas, even though it did invoke a notion of freedom of the press. This shouldn't be surprising. Why should Colonials with a relatively limited experience of popular printed debate believe in a modern marketplace of ideas? Why should they embrace a metaphor of public communication that sees the common good emerging (almost magically) from the vigorous self-interested competition of opposing parties and classes? And why should people assume that speech is a kind of behavior whose turpitude and foul effects cannot be punished like other behaviors?

Surveys show that, after a couple hundred years' experience with free political debate and an intense half-century of publicity campaigns by media, politicians, lawyers and academics, an alarming percentage of the population still fails to embrace a libertarian conception of freedom of the press. Fortunately, popular attitudes are kept in check by a civil liberties elite. But this elite didn't always exist.

If 18th- and early 19th-century Americans believed less in the press than we do, they believed more in the crowd. In the old Anglo-American tradition of political action, riots claimed legitimacy as the spontaneous, righteous expression of the people. This claim distinguishes a pattern of behavior that we can call majoritarian violence. It was this tradition of crowd action that justified the mobbing of Loyalists during the Revolution. The same rationale was applied frequently during the 19th century.

The abolition controversy provides a host of examples. In the mid-1830s, a movement demanding immediate end to slavery grew in the Northern states. Using the techniques of evangelical revivalists—including emotional speeches, pamphlets, picture cards and newspapers—anti-slavery activists launched a national campaign of agitation. Their opponents countered with traditional crowd actions. Much of this action was symbolic, something like a ritual—such as pelting speakers with rotten eggs. Some of it was much less benign.

Dozens of abolitionist papers were mobbed. One editor, Elijah Lovejoy of the Alton, Ill., *Observer,* was killed. Anti-abolitionist rioters often inflicted considerable collateral damage, too. The mob that attacked the *Philanthropist* in Cincinnati in 1836 celebrated its destruction of that paper's office and equipment by burning down the city's African-American neighborhood.

The *Philanthropist* riot speaks eloquently about the accepted role of printed discourse in the early Republic. In a city full of newspapers, only one editor defended the right of the *Philanthropist* to openly champion emancipation, and he changed his mind in mid-riot. Cincinnati's civic leaders blamed the victim for causing unrest and embarrassing the city.

What is remarkable in this episode was the collusion of leaders of both political parties. One needn't look very hard to understand why. Both national parties consisted of coalitions of state factions; both needed to convince their Southern wings that they were sound on the slavery question.

The anti-abolitionist riots of the 1830s and 1840s were just a skirmish compared to the Civil War. The military war between North and South generated a political war inside the North. Crowds menaced or attacked more than 100 Northern newspapers, almost all Democratic—and therefore prone to be critical of President Abraham Lincoln, a Republican. Such incidents took place mostly during election campaigns; too often to be coincidental, the mobs included soldiers on leave from the Union Army.

The Civil War ended an era of violence against the press. Never again would mainstream partisan papers be the targets of mobs. And rarely would journals of opinion run by respectable men be attacked. Americans had come to accept a notion of politics as a marketplace. In a marketplace of ideas, as in any other market, it was appropriate for people of means to seek self-interest, and there was no need for intervention because impersonal mechanisms will insure fairness. Free expression of unpopular ideas seemed a lot less dangerous now—in fact, conflating politics with the marketplace seems to have devalued ideas generally. In this way, a realm of freedom was staked out—for some.

Majoritarian crowd actions didn't end, but instead they came to target social groups—the media of racial and linguistic minorities, and labor papers.

Again, the journalist victims were accused of threatening public safety. When a series of African-American editors, including Ida B. Wells, was mobbed for criticizing lynching, civic leaders blamed them for stirring up race hatred, and even for encouraging black men to rape white women. Likewise, activist labor journalists were accused of threatening the freedom of workers to contract as individuals. During World War I, German-language publications were accused of undermining the war effort.

This catalog of oppressions will sound whiny to some. It sounds whiny to me, and for a simple reason: The press was hardly in the front line in any of these battles. Only a few Loyalist printers were mobbed, while a great many clergy, lawyers and ordinary citizens were targeted. No Loyalist editor was actually tarred and feathered, much less killed. One abolitionist editor was killed, while millions of slaves suffered untold cruelties. No African-American editor was actually lynched. The sufferings of labor journalists are dwarfed by those of the men and women on the picket line.

Special pleading aside, then, we should note that the press has suffered violence on behalf of others suffering more. This is something to be proud of, not something to whine about. We should be alarmed if it is no longer the case.

By the end of the 19th century, though, most mainstream publications had defined themselves not as advocates but as retailers. They retailed stories to people, and then retailed their readers to advertisers, who then retailed goods to these same readers. These commercial media rarely encountered majoritarian violence. To be sure, in an epoch of tremendous head-to-head competition in media markets, reporters were encouraged to be aggressive and editors outspoken—and they did get beaten up. They were assaulted by aggrieved individuals, though, not by mobs.

Today's mainstream American reporters and editors don't encounter this kind of attack either. It's not that there are no aggressive or outspoken journalists. But even the aggressive ones are careful to detach their personalities from the stories they tell; they put on the armor of professionalism and objectivity. The attributed quotation is a sword and the balancing expert opinion a shield.

The result is that good journalists, no matter how often bylined or how regularly televised, are somehow anonymous to the public. Even the journalists the public recognizes—such as Mike Wallace and George Will—are on TV and not on Main Street, where you could beat them up. Not that anyone wants to beat up George Will—though I do know people who would like to put thumbprints on his glasses.

The public seems to accept opining as something the George Wills of the world are supposed to do. And the pundits respond by opining without much force of personality. Even Rush Limbaugh, the most inexhaustible of the lot, is not in the same league as earlier windbags. Today's pundits—even Limbaugh—are professionals, experts, above the fray in some fashion: They deny their partisan allegiances even while proclaiming them. And when professionalism fails to protect today's press, the police do.

The exception is immigrant journalists, who remain frequent targets of violent assault, as another essay in this volume points out. Most of these seem to come from political conflicts inside immigrant communities that are not yet fully acculturated to mainstream news routines. These attacks are little noticed by the general public, who are unaware of even the most prominent immigrant journalists. In fact, it is the unconcern of the mainstream that is most remarkable— these attacks receive relatively little publicity, and the attackers have mostly escaped arrest.

Professionalism surely insulates journalists from some hostility, but it also invites new kinds of hostility and violence that comes in three identifiable types.

The first, inclusionary violence, is when people who feel underrepresented by the news media use violence to force a change in the news menu. This, of course, is what terrorists are often accused of, though the media themselves (at least in the United States) have rarely been the targets of terrorist attacks. When the Unabomber got the *New York Times* and *Washington Post* to print his manifesto, he did so by threatening to blow up third parties. A few years ago I expected inclusionary violence to increase, but it seems that the Internet has worked as a safety valve, allowing abundant expression of marginalized ideas and information in a setting where little action will result.

The second type of violence is eyes-of-a-nation hostility. It occurs when reporters turning the eyes of a nation on a reticent place or group, and the objects of scrutiny try to avert the eyes of the nation by attacking the reporters. This is the kind of violence that struck Don Bolles and many national reporters covering the civil rights movement in the South. In the case of Southern segregationists, this strategy backfired;

it hasn't been tried on a large scale since, though white supremacists have been known to discourage media attention.

Eyes-of-a-nation violence was usually the strategy of well-organized local elite groups. The growth sector in hostility toward the press these days, though, is with the politically disfranchised and disenchanted, especially on the right. And this movement seems truly bottom-up.

Much as liberals might want to blame mainstream pundits and Republican chieftains for the current rash of far-right violence, the activists seem to be really divorced from the mainstream right. Rather, they are hooked up to their own network of computer bulletin boards, publishers, small bookstores and face-to-face forums. These disaffected lumpens seem to be producing a hostility less strategic than expressive in its intent.

If there is to be a new wave of violence against the news media in the United States, I think it will come from the angry grass roots. It might come from the far right, where there is already a well-articulated critique of the liberal biases, moral corrosiveness and conspiratorial ownership of corporate media that connects them with an oppressive, even bloody power structure. In Oklahoma City, it was a federal office building that was bombed, but the same impulse could well have targeted CBS. A similar logic is available at the other end of the political spectrum. During the Los Angeles riots following the Rodney King verdict, the *Los Angeles Times* was targeted because rioters identified it with a racist power structure.

Of course the *Times* wasn't much hurt. Nor has CBS been bombed. History shows that the U.S. media are safer now than ever before from physical attack. But they will never be entirely safe. In an age with any political action at all, good journalists should expect some friction. There is great honor in facing danger for the right reasons.

John Nerone has taught communications at the University of Illinois since 1983. He is author of Violence Against the Press: Policing the Public Sphere in U.S. History.

19

Repairing the Damage

Ed Kelley

American editors directing coverage of episodic violence in their hometowns are beginning to recognize a small set of victims within their newsrooms—their own journalists who are unable to cope with what they have witnessed.

Think about it: Emergency workers, medical personnel and law enforcement officers who confront the bodies of people blown apart by an explosion are encouraged to seek counseling for "critical incident stress." But journalists, who view the same horrors and suffer the same stress, are rarely urged to find help in coping with what they have seen.

The culture of most news organizations discourages reporters, photographers and others—trained as they are to stand firm and unaffected amidst chaos—from making themselves comfortable enough to discuss psychological damage. In most newsrooms, "debriefing" journalists in a professional way after they view a traumatic event is barely an afterthought, much less a priority.

The results of such negligence vary widely, depending on the story and its extent. But the signals eventually could surface, even if it is months after the episode.

A solution: Voluntary and unobtrusive counseling by outside professionals. It was used in our newsroom, following the bombing of the federal building in Oklahoma City last year, and remains in place for a small group, which meets periodically with Charlotte Lankard, a licensed counselor who strongly encourages assistance for journalists perched in or near scenes of violence. One state where that is formally encouraged and practiced is in Michigan; there, an innovative program, run by Michigan State University's School of Journalism in East Lansing, is designed to help news organizations cope with coverage of human cruelty.

To be sure, the circumstances of journalistic trauma incurred close to home are very different from the dangers of journalists who risk their lives daily in the world's hot spots. Nothing in the craft equates to being attacked, shot at or tortured while seeking information for often unappreciative audiences in democracies halfway around the world.

Still, city desk reporters are prone to share some of the psychological, if not physical, scars of their overseas counterparts.

As the senior news executive who directed coverage of the Oklahoma City bombing for hometown readers, I relied on a veteran staff of largely homegrown talent that fought its rawest emotions for weeks while trying to make sense of one of the biggest crimes ever committed on American soil.

The bombing took its toll on our city and state. It also took a toll on our newspaper staff.

The wife of one of our pressmen died in the blast. A cousin of one of our reporters died, too; he wrote her obituary. Most of the people who died were federal employees, and more than a few of them were news sources for some of our reporters. Our first reporter on the scene, who arrived within 10 minutes of the blast, was a childhood friend of one of those killed. A Secret Service agent who died was a reporter's neighbor. One reporter had tried, unsuccessfully, to convince a young government lawyer to meet for a date. The lawyer died in the blast.

Three members of our newsroom were in the area at the time of the explosion. One reporter, across the street at the post office, was injured. Another reporter, in a nearby building with officials from a county grand jury, was badly shaken. And one of our graphic artists was seen on television running from another day-care center in the area, with two young boys—one of them his year-old son—under his arms.

Is it any wonder, then, that the grief was so deep and unnatural for a newsroom accustomed, like all American newspapers, to trying to filter its work through a dispassionate lens?

If there is one image I take from the events of April 1995 and beyond, it is that of journalists at our newspaper wiping away tears and clearing their throats, then pushing forth to report, write, photograph, edit and create. No doubt there were similar feelings in newsrooms all over the world on the day of the bombing. But it is doubtful they could have been as intense as they were just a few miles away from the blast site. As journalists, we were covering our victims in our town. We did so without ever being in harm's way, but our task was no less grim, or less difficult, because of the setting.

The emotions would be the same for any news organization covering violence or disasters in their backyard. Caught in the swirl of a huge story on deadline, top editors and news managers are not likely to see the psychological damage. Reporters, photographers and assignment editors use the urgency and adrenaline of the moment to subconsciously postpone the mental toll. (One of our reporters, a woman with a heart condition, began hyperventilating soon after the explosion. She thought she was having a heart attack but didn't tell her editors, thinking they would pull her off the story.)

Some staffers exposed to violence will remain in the newsroom, even after deadline, because the camaraderie allows them to avoid dealing with their feelings. "I didn't want to go home and be alone," one veteran reporter told me in the bombing's aftermath.

Lankard, the counselor, was in our newsroom within a few hours of the bombing, recruited by the newspaper's human resources director to meet with anyone and everyone who wanted to discuss what had happened. She has returned weekly since then to meet with staffers who want to talk through emotions rubbed raw by the story. She also was involved in formal discussions with rescue workers and medical professionals who were at the bombing scene and hospitals.

Judy Kuhlman, a cityside reporter who was among the first journalists at the scene, said she suffered from violent nightmares for months after the bombing. Kuhlman credits Lankard's assistance for easing the trauma. The counseling, Kuhlman said, "helps you get on with your life." Charolette Aiken, another reporter who met regularly with Lankard, said the sessions helped the group "identify what was bomb-related stress and what was normal stress."

Said Lankard: "Journalists are taught to put their feelings aside...but they never go back and debrief and talk about their feelings." That's especially true in the typical newsroom hierarchy, created years ago by men whose not-so-subtle message in stressful situations was, as Lankard said, for "everybody to take care of your own business. Don't bring it into the newsroom."

But journalists' emotions are in the newsroom, even if they are not readily seen. Covering violence makes it difficult to cope with what Lankard described as the "unfinished business" of the past that often surfaces in people during stressful situations. News professionals also feel particularly unappreciated as they go about their work in the aftermath of a disaster. While others in the community volunteer for a variety of chores, from giving blood to feeding caregivers, journalists must remain detached. As one reporter told me, "I remember thinking what I was doing after the bombing wasn't that useful, that I wanted to do some hands-on work."

For those who do not get help early on, emotional aftershocks may appear days or months after a traumatic episode. The signals fall into four areas, according to the International Critical Incident Stress Foundation:

• Physical, such as fatigue, chest pain, headaches, grinding of teeth and fainting.

• Cognitive, such as confusion, poor concentration, memory loss and nightmares.

• Emotional, such as anxiety, denial, depression and intense anger.

• Behavioral, such as change in appetite, withdrawal, change in speech and alcohol consumption.

The differences in how the sexes work through stress are especially apparent in the open environment of a newsroom. Today, a handful of staffers at our newspaper still meet regularly with Lankard. Aside from the first few days, all in Lankard's group are women.

"Women who received help for what they saw received some backlash," reporter Aiken said. How many men sought counseling is not known; my guess is it was less than a half-dozen or so. "I think guys tend to think they can deal with this, but I know men who are having problems with it," reporter Kuhlman said. Aiken thinks debriefing sessions should have been mandatory for reporters, editors and photographers, much like it was for law enforcement officials who worked at the bomb site and with victims.

Men and women alike in our newsroom talk among themselves about how relationships in their lives have changed—not necessarily for the better—or how they are more emotional, whether crying more often in a movie theater or around their children. Lankard warns that it might take years, but the psychological damage to journalists from chronicling violence could prompt marriage breakups, substance abuse and serious mental problems. But is what happened in Oklahoma City peculiar only to our newspaper? The Associated Press's bureau across town, swelled with correspondents from other postings to cover the bombing, reported no formal requests for counseling, although one staffer sought private help.

On a larger scale, neither the AP nor Reuters have formal policies in place to routinely debrief their respective employees who are placed in or near violent circumstances at home or abroad. But both organizations handle requests for help as employees express the need. The AP's benefits plan covers mental health needs, and there is a hotline for staffers to use if problems arise at home or on the job. Still, as an AP official noted, "it's a tricky situation; obviously, you can't force people into counseling."

At Michigan State University, the School of Journalism, with funding from Michigan's W. A. Dart Foundation, established its Victims and Media Program in 1991 to help journalists address issues created when covering victims of violence. Besides workshops and seminars on how to approach and interview victims, the program also offers news organizations structured opportunities for debriefing and discussion of the challenges posed in covering incidents of violence and horror.

The Victims and Media Program response team, for example, visited the local newspaper in Ludington, Mich., after a devastating apartment fire left several children dead. The team has an agreement with the Michigan Press Association to provide on-site counseling services for member news organizations. Efforts also are under way to offer one-on-one peer counseling in person and through electronic mail and telephone calls.

Perhaps it is the hometown backdrop of journalists struggling to remain detached as their community is ravaged by a violent act that makes the psychological damage more acute. But for American news organizations, the bombing in Oklahoma City and the explosions that rocked TWA Flight 800 and the Atlanta Olympics last summer should be a wake-up call. Journalists can be wounded, often seriously, even without being in the proverbial line of fire. Those of us who direct coverage owe them a chance to be made whole again.

Ed Kelley is managing editor of the Daily Oklahoman *in Oklahoma City.*

20

Watch Your Back

John Owen

There is one undeniable conclusion buried in the depressing accounts of attacks on the press compiled by the Committee to Protect Journalists (CPJ): namely, that anyone can murder a journalist and get away with it.

Rarely do news organizations have a clear idea of who is behind the death of a reporter or camera crew. Often the murders take place in countries where contract killings are commonplace, and there are thousands of unsolved murders of ordinary citizens. In Russia, for example, CPJ reported recently that while there have been 13 unsolved murders of journalists in the past two years, there were 8,000 unsolved murders of Russians in 1995.

But when a news organization does think it knows who murdered its journalist, what can and should it do? The BBC struggled with that issue when one of its talented young journalists, John Schofield, was murdered in Croatia in August 1995.

Like so many assignments that turn dangerous, there was no early warning signal that the BBC team need fear for their safety. They had the story all to themselves. They had broken free from the international pack, days after the Croatian army had expelled Serbian families from the bitterly contested enclave known as the Krajina. They had no "minders" (the derogatory name for government censors) to restrict their movements or stop them from recording what they saw. They had already recorded enough exclusive news material to give them a world scoop. Now on their hillside perch, they had an excellent vantage point to observe the burning of homes—new evidence that the Croatian military had committed what amounted to ethnic cleansing.

The BBC unit was outside of its unmarked, white armored vehicle. BBC World Service cameraman Adam Kelleher had his camera mounted on a tripod and was recording billows of smoke from the burning houses in the distance. World Service reporter Jonathan Birchell and Arabic Service reporter Inwar Asawi were watching and waiting. BBC Radio reporter Schofield was recording his own eyewitness account that would give his edited piece a dramatic sense of urgency.

What the BBC team didn't know was that they were being tracked by as many as a dozen Croatian soldiers who were hidden from view in the cornfields below them. Suddenly and without warning shots rang out. The soldiers, more than a football field away from the BBC, had fired their AK-47s directly at them. There was silence, then a second round of shooting.

Three of the BBC team were hit but not hurt badly. Schofield was not so lucky. He lay motionless on the ground.

Cameraman Kelleher had the presence of mind to put his hands up in the air and then walk toward the soldiers shouting in English: "We're journalists! We're journalists!" That gesture, that appearance of a surrender, was persuasive enough for the commanding officer to come out of hiding. After a conversation, the officer called for a field ambulance, and within minutes an army doctor arrived.

But it was too late for Schofield. He was dead. Not even his requisitioned BBC flak jacket could save him.

British and U.S. newspapers reported the killing of Schofield. Both the *New York Times* and *the British Independent* quoted an unnamed Croatian government official as saying that "rebel Serbs" had killed Schofield. The BBC and British diplomats were reported as saying that the shots had come from Croatian troops who were "nervous and jumpy" because a busload of Croatian soldiers had been attacked the day before, very close to the spot where the BBC team was recording pictures.

The BBC never wavered in its view that Croatian troops had committed what Ray Gowdridge of the BBC termed "unprovoked murder." But Gowdridge, the BBC's senior news executive assigned to investigate the case, still had to explain what his unaccompanied news team was doing reporting in a contested area that the Croatians had declared off-limits to the media. Besides, the Croatians, even after conceding that it wasn't the Krajina Serbs who were responsible, still tried to absolve the Croatian army and concocted half a dozen theories to explain why the BBC had been fired upon.

As of this writing, nearly a year after Schofield's shooting, the Croatian authorities have yet to produce a report—despite repeated assurances to both the BBC and the British Embassy in Zagreb that an inquiry had been conducted. Indeed, the British Embassy in Zagreb insists that Ambassador Gavin Hewitt bring up the subject at every occasion where the Croatian Minister for Defense, Gojko Susak, is present.

If the Croatians have concluded their investigation, they are not saying.

For veteran BBC correspondent Martin Bell, whose courageous reporting in the former Yugoslavia nearly cost him his life (Bell was wounded by shrapnel from mortar fire in August of 1992), there was never any doubt about who was responsible for Schofield's death: "I have had my own discussions with the Croatian army on this issue. They're very hard-line. They accept no responsibility. Their feeling is that by putting up a wall the issue will go away. Clearly, the issue has gone away."

Perhaps, but perhaps not.

Gowdridge rejects any suggestion that the BBC has remained silent. He insists that in his view, "the diplomatic pressure that the Foreign Office has put on through the Embassy is the most likely way of finding the results of the inquiries into what caused the incident."

Peter Preston, the longtime editor of the British newspaper *The Guardian* and now chairman of the International Press Institute, won't second-guess the BBC's approach. But Preston does identify what he calls "levers" that the BBC and other press organizations might operate. "Clearly, Croatia does want to be a member of the Council of Europe because that is a sort of stamp of approval and puts it in the holding zone for the European Union at some stage. And it's sensible that as that stamp of approval is given, that the government's attitude to human rights, in particular press rights, is held up to the microscope."

In London this past May, Susan Schofield, the widow of John Schofield, joined the families of other slain journalists at the official opening of The Freedom Forum's new European Center. She brought along her nearly 3-month-old baby daughter Charlotte. Shortly after John Schofield was murdered, Susan discovered that she was pregnant with their first child. Baby Charlotte was born on Easter.

The death of Schofield, like the deaths of far too many journalists around the world, has jolted news organizations into examining whether some stories are too dangerous to cover. Instead of sending their own staff correspondents or crews, assignment editors now debate whether they should rely more heavily on free-lancers.

But what responsibilities do news organizations have to free-lancers if they get killed or hurt badly? It's a subject that has escaped the attention of many news executives.

For free-lancers who are hungry to make money and secure their reputations, there have never been so many potential assignments in war zones and nasty ethnic conflicts. More and more, the most dangerous work falls to free-lancers. This trend worries the BBC's Bell: "We reached the point in Chechnya with people I call cowboys who do things under fire for a living—taking risks which other people won't take. They do all the serious stuff while the network correspondents go in with staff crews and do a piece to camera, get a few shots and then nip out. I don't think that we should do it."

Television news makes the most use of free-lancers. Cameramen like Rory Peck have made dangerous assignments their specialty. He and his wife, Juliet Peck, gravitated to places where "important things happened." That's why they decided to move to Moscow in 1992. "He was hugely demanded by the different television companies," Juliet explained. "And whenever anything was going on, they would ring us up and say, 'We understand that the Abkazians are having an offensive against the Georgians, or such and such is going on in Ngorno-Karabach or wherever and will you go?'"

Rory and Juliet were in Georgia in October 1993 when plotters tried to overthrow President Boris Yeltsin. A German network tracked down Peck and hired him to work in Moscow covering the turbulent events.

When the rebels decided to attack the headquarters of the state television broadcaster, Ostankino, the government troops were inside ready to retaliate. Peck, along with scores of international crews, stood outside waiting for the confrontation. But Peck got trapped in a lethal cross fire and was killed.

For Juliet, it meant coming to terms for the second time with the death of a journalist-husband (her first husband, a still photographer, was murdered in Pakistan). But she channeled her grief into a cause. She created, with the help of family and good friends of hers and Rory's, a trust fund to commemorate his work and to honor other outstanding free-lancers and filmmakers. The first award was presented last year to a Russian cameraman, Vachad Karamov, posthumously. Karamov had been killed covering the Chechen conflict.

The Rory Peck Trust Fund was also established to help support the dependents of slain free-lancers. Juliet was painfully aware of the financial hardships. She was grateful for the one-time cash award—the equivalent of $50,000—from the German network that had hired Rory to shoot in Moscow. But Rory, like so many free-lancers, was not covered by the kind of comprehensive war insurance policy that news organizations purchase for their staff journalists.

Through the help of generous friends, Juliet has been able to care for her blended family of six children. She is quick to note, however, that survivors—mostly widows—of free-lancers in developing countries are often left with few means of support.

Juliet Peck and others involved in the Trust Fund have devoted enormous time and energy to laying the groundwork for an international free-lancers' insurance fund. If they can enlist the support of huge umbrella groups such as the International Federation of Journalists—with a membership of nearly half a million whose dues could create a pool of insurance—then free-lancers and their families can take on risky assignments knowing that their own families are protected. The plan is probably a year or two away from fruition.

Until that happens, many free-lancers will accept assignments from respected news organizations and assume that their families will be looked after if they are killed or disabled. Such assumptions are likely to lead to disappointment.

What angers Peck most is the "really grubby" business of news bosses who duck responsibility after giving verbal assurances that they will take care of the free-lancer's survivors. According to Peck, the free-lance world still revolves around verbal trust and old friendships, neither of which are legally binding.

Journalists of the caliber of John Schofield and Rory Peck will never stop taking risks to get to the story. There is no such thing, the author Phillip Knightley reminds us, as "anodyne journalism."

News organizations must then take the necessary steps, large or small, to contribute to the overall protection of journalists. One killer, be it a mobster or trigger-happy soldier, brought to justice for murdering a journalist sends a signal that it is no longer open season on reporters and camera men and women.

And if the news organization champions all journalists, staff and free-lance, then the journalistic community at large is strengthened.

John Owen, director of The Freedom Forum's European Center, was most recently chief of foreign bureaus and London bureau chief for the Canadian Broadcasting Corp.

Part VIII

Interviews

21

Reporting from War Zones

W.C. Heinz, war correspondent,
interviewed by George Robinson

Several of us went up in a jeep in a small town in Germany. A mortar shell came in on my side and hit a wall to the left of me. I remember the hot flame and orange color. I had a splinter in my left cheek and another in my left hand.

Then I knew what it would be like to get killed, because that would be the last thing you would know, if you were killed by artillery or a mortar. You would hear this noise and see this orange color and it would be very hot.

We had the best duty of war correspondents anywhere. Once they got off the beaches, we could always get into some kind of a house or a barn. And we had the press camps, which were not too far removed from the front lines most of the time. We could go up 10 or 15 miles to the front and come back. It was the best duty in the war for anybody. We didn't have to salute anybody, literally or figuratively, only those we thought deserved it.

Q: What went into the decision to go in harm's way?

It was a question of how far you wanted to go. You wanted to come back alive, but you wanted to do your job.

How have you been doing lately, that's what I used to think. You wouldn't want to do this every day. But if you had been back of the front lines for a while, you felt morally obligated and professionally obligated to go up and see something again.

When you first went out and you were new you had the idea that it might happen to somebody else, but it wouldn't happen to you. But

147

after you'd seen it happen rather close by you'd realize that but for a split second it could be you.

Then you became more calculating as to where you went.... You'd go along as far as you had the balls to. I didn't have the balls every day.

Q: In a combat situation, what were you thinking about? Were you taking notes, literally or mentally?

What you're really thinking about is staying alive. You're not writing the piece in your mind, you're getting what you can without getting hurt. And when you get back you're awfully glad you did, because an awful lot of guys didn't.

We had 30 guys with us in the press corps, and I'd say, maybe a half a dozen I looked up to. The other guys might be nice guys, but I didn't think they were doing the job.

Q: What kept you going on a day-to-day basis?

You just couldn't leave the GIs alone. I mean, they were doing the fighting. They were my age. Once in a while I would run into a guy who I knew in New York when I was covering the streets, who was now in the Army.

We came back every day and they stayed up there. I've never forgotten that all my life.... I've been overburdened with empathy, but it's good for a reporter. I certainly had it for the GIs. It's amazing what they went through....

All the time you realized you had better material on a daily basis than you would ever have again in your life.... There are rewards. But I owe it all to the ones who got crippled, the ones who died, the ones who stayed there.

W. C. Heinz covered the European theater of WWII, from D-Day to V-E Day for the New York Sun. *He was present at the Normandy invasion, the Battle of the Bulge and the bridgeheat at Remagen. After he returned to the States he enjoyed a lengthy career as a newspaper and magazine writer and book author.*

George Robinson, an author and free-lance writer based in New York, is co-chair of the National Writers Union national book campaign.

22

Kemal Kurspahic

Kemal Kurspahic, editor of a Sarajevo daily,
interviewed by George Robinson

Our building was targeted in the first few days of the siege. We faced a number of obstacles. You can't bring a roll of newsprint into the city when it's besieged. There is no security for the approach to the building. You lose your phone connections. Later we lost our electricity. I don't think there has ever been a paper in the history of journalism that published for three and a half years under such conditions.

We had the newsroom in a series of atom bomb shelters that according to old Yugoslav law all companies had to have in their basements. We moved the editorial offices and newsroom into that basement.

In order to reduce the risks of the coming and going of the staff, I organized work in seven-day shifts. A team of experts and journalists would come in on Monday and stay for seven days in what I called the newsroom/bedroom. We had cots for up to 10 people.

We addressed the shortage of newsprint by reducing the number of pages and circulation. But the siege lasted longer than anyone could expect.

The first year of the siege we changed our size 13 times, using all kinds of newsprint, any paper you could find in the city. We had to change color four times, using the cheapest paper available—pinkish, yellowish, bluish, greenish. We had to reduce circulation lower and lower—12,000, 8, 6, then 2,000 copies. At that point it became a security problem because people started fighting for their copies of the paper.

For many months of the siege, we were the only source of news in the city. There was no electricity to watch television or listen to the radio. And when we printed even 2,000 copies the readership was much larger because people shared the same copy of the paper. It was a precious commodity in the city, actually the only commodity in the city for many days. There were just bread and the paper, and there were many days without bread.

Q: Why keep going through all this?

When the shooting started and our building was hit, I had an editorial staff meeting. And at that point I told them that we should continue for at least three reasons.

One was our vision of the paper: It started during the Nazi occupation during the Second World War, as an opposition paper for the partisans in the mountains. So we had a tradition of fighting for certain principles and freedom, and we were approaching the 50th anniversary of the paper.

Then there was the profession. I felt that if hundreds of foreign journalists could come and cover the war and the siege of Sarajevo, then we, whose city, whose country, whose families were here, shouldn't just give up and withdraw in the face of the terror.

Third was a responsibility to our readers. In the last few years of Communist rule, the paper gained some trust among the public and some credibility by advocating political reforms and by opposing the nationalistic parties which won elections in Bosnia in 1990. They wanted to control the media the way the Communists did and appoint editors according to the views of the parties. We refused that and had a constitutional court case and won. So there was the feeling that the trust we gained meant that we should continue doing what we were doing.

I offered anyone who was scared for their lives and families an opportunity to leave Sarajevo, to leave the paper, and actually no one wanted to do that. We evacuated a few women with children, put them on the last bus out of the city. Everyone else stayed....

I believe that our continuing publication was encouragement to the ordinary people under the siege. On June 10, 1992, the third month of the siege, our building was set afire by artillery fire. It was burning all night. At that time we still had electricity in Sarajevo, so people could see the building burning.

No one was expecting a newspaper to come out of those flames the next morning. The fire was extinguished at 6 a.m. and five minutes later all presses started. We had prepared the paper in that bomb shelter.

People were celebrating the appearance of the paper that day. It was a source of hope, people seeing the paper coming out of those flames, out of that madness.

We had some losses. People got killed on duty. The first journalist killed in the Bosnian war was our small-town correspondent in Zvornik, the town that first came under attack of Serbian forces coming from Serbia. Our correspondent knew he was facing death. (The day before he put his family on a truck with people fleeing the advances of the Serbian forces.) But he stayed in the town to report and to die reporting from his office. He was found there and killed. We learned maybe two or three weeks later from a woman who called his family and said that she saw him being dragged by the legs out of the doors and buried in a mass grave.

Our photography editor was killed in July 1992 in the center of Sarajevo, taking pictures of people waiting for water. We had a financial clerk killed on a bus between our offices and the city center, on her way home from work. There were many people wounded.

I often thought about the risks that we took. I think we did not take more risks than ordinary people in Sarajevo. People got killed just waiting for water. Children got killed playing in their neighborhoods. Doing our job we just took the same risks as everyone under siege.

On the other hand, I believe that having so many things to do, so many problems to solve in order to have the paper, just being busy for the survival of the paper and our own survival, we did not have much time to think about the milieu surrounding us. It was a kind of mental shield against the misery of the people. That's the way that we faced the danger.

Kemal Kurspahic is the U.S. editor-correspondent of Oslobodjenje, *the independent daily newspaper of Sarajevo, and was editor in chief during the first two years of the city's siege.*

23

Civil Unrest

Bob Greene, investigative reporter,
interviewed by George Robinson

There were times covering the civil rights movement when you were just scared shitless.... One of my ultimate scares was in Philadelphia, Miss., when those three young men [Michael Schwerner, James Chaney and Andrew Goodman] were killed.

That night I was passing through Meridian,...and I stopped into SNCC headquarters. It was maybe 9 o'clock at night.

I said, "What's going on?"

"Well, we're a little worried, these three guys haven't come back. They went up to Philadelphia. And we're really scared."

I said, "Maybe they're off having dinner."

"No, we have a code. We've got reports that a black church got burned and we know the sheriff's department is involved in it. We know they got stopped for speeding by a deputy sheriff up there."

So I called my desk and told them what was going on and my editor said, "Oh, just go up there and knock on doors." I said, "Al, you don't just go up there and knock on doors at this time of night. You'll get shot."

So the next morning, I went up to the courthouse in Philadelphia. And Claude Sitton and Karl Fleming are also there. The three of us are standing there in the hallway of the courthouse. The sheriff has come back from Meridian, where he had been the night before; it was the deputy sheriff who had done all this stuff. And we're talking to the sheriff. And he's telling us, "There's nothing wrong. My deputy says there's nothing wrong."

"Well, can we just talk to the deputy, can we see the report, the tickets?"

All of a sudden he walks into his office and slams the door. We look down the hall and there must be 25, 30 people standing there and looking at us, staring at us.

And one of them says to us, "Where you from?"

"We're just here doing our job."

"You from Philadelphia?"

"No."

"You from Neshoba County?"

"No."

"You from the state of Mississippi?"

"No."

"What's yo' job?"

"Newspapermen."

"You Yankee newspapermen?"

"We're just newspapermen doing our job."

"You Yankee newspapermen? Get outta here."

"Well, we can't get out of here, we're just trying to do a job."

"Okay fellas, we tole 'em!"

And they start moving towards us. I go out one door, Fleming goes out another door, Sitton goes out a third door and goes running across the street. Turner Catledge was managing editor for the *Times* at that time. A relative of his had a store there. Sitton goes running in and the guy says, "Just go running out the back. You can't stay here."

I got in my car, a rented Lincoln. I took off. I went to the farm that had been burnt down. I interviewed the folks there, and they identified the deputy sheriff as one of the persons who had done the burning of the church. I got affidavits from them.

As I come out of this dirt road, there's this pickup truck with Confederate flags flying and about eight people standing in the back, hanging on. Now, I don't know if that thing was chasing me or not, but I took off for Jackson [Miss.] at about 100 mph, and this thing was following me for at least 15, 16 miles. I just kept going to Jackson and filed my story.

Maybe the danger was real, maybe not. I think the danger was real, because those three kids turned up dead.

Q: What keeps you going in a situation like that?

I don't want to sound pretentious, but when my generation was going into the business, we went into it because it was an opportunity to effect change for good. You never did it for money, because you knew it was the poorest paying job in the world. In 1948 I was making $23.50 a week in Jersey City.

But you went in because No. 1 it's challenging. No. 2, you can effect change, you can try to work for what is presumed to be good, if nothing else, by bringing accurate information to people.

Part of what keeps you going is you're already committed to the thing, and you understand that when you do this, if you kick somebody in the kneecap, somebody is going to kick you in the kneecap back.

I mean, I ended up being audited as part of the Nixon enemies thing; John Dean said he went over to the IRS and personally arranged to have my taxes audited.

I hate to admit it, but there's also a certain element of thrill. There's a rush: How can I get around them and get that story home?

Bob Greene, a journalism professor at Hofstra University, was an investigative reporter for the Jersey Journal *and* Newsday *for over 40 years. He headed up the Investigative Reporters and Editors Inc. task force in Arizona after the murder of Don Bolles.*

24

Organized Crime

Maria Caballero, Colombian investigative reporter,
interviewed by George Robinson

It's very interesting in Colombia, but it's also very dangerous. I have to work on very difficult, dangerous issues such as drug trafficking and politicians involved in corruption. Hot issues.

You receive a lot of calls and messages telling you that you are going to die or your family will be killed if you publish anything on different issues. This is very common. It's a daily source of stress.

I decided that if I paid attention to each of those phone calls and messages, I could not do anything. I decided that if they're going to kill me, okay, kill me. But I have to work and I have a responsibility here.

I have to forget my own security in order to work on the issues that I work on here.

I worry about my reporters and I talk with them before I send them out on a dangerous assignment. If it is very dangerous, I prefer to do it by myself.

One month ago I had an interview with the son of leader of the Cali cartel. I had to go alone to meet with him in a very isolated place. It's the only way you can talk with sources who are dangerous—in very isolated places outside the cities. I knew that anything could happen. They have "disappeared" a lot of people.

I went to Uraba, it's a very special place. There are guerrillas, people who are wanted by the security forces, paramilitary outfits fighting the guerrillas, sometimes military forces working with the paramilitary forces, drug-traffickers—whatever else you can imagine. And to go there you know that you can disappear and no one will ever know who killed you.

Everyone is an enemy there. If they see a strange person, they assume you're a spy. But I have been lucky. They haven't killed me up to now.

Q: What keeps you going day to day?
This country is very special. You live in danger everywhere. Ever since I was a little girl I wanted to know how people can be so violent. Why kill? Why are things the way they are here? How do these people think?

Through journalism I have tried to find answers. I talk with every kind of person. I have a lot of sources among the drug traffickers, a lot of sources in the police forces, a lot of sources in the military forces— a lot of sources everywhere.

The best policy is to be in touch with them, but not to be friends with them. I call them, I meet with them. I always say, "I'm not saying I will publish anything, but I want to understand what is happening." I'll continue working on these issues because it's the only way to understand what is happening here.

Maria Caballero is special investigations editor/national editor for the Colombian newsweekly Cambio 16. *She was a Nieman Fellow at Harvard University for the 1996–1997 academic year.*

25

Portfolio

Donna Ferrato, photojournalist,
interviewed by George Robinson

I almost left and didn't come back after a Christmas Eve party where the kids were doing drugs, Mafiosi were dealing cocaine, kids were smashing through the walls. I was having bizarre conversations with Mafia guys. It was scary. I was eight months pregnant, and I decided to stay away from these people.

But a few months later I got a call from the wife, who said her husband had become very threatening and had a gun. She asked me to come back so I could see what was going on. So I did.

When I saw her I was shocked by how much weight she had lost and how bad she looked. I said, "I think you are doing too many drugs."

She ended up hiding whatever drugs she could find, and it was that day when I first saw him attack her. Outside, he tried to drag her into the house to find his drugs.

She was crying, the children were screaming and crying, and I picked up the camera and took his picture, thinking it would make him stop and it did. He disappeared and we didn't see him the rest of the day.

That night I woke up to hear her screaming again. I ran downstairs to the bathroom and found him attacking her, destroying the bathroom, the bedroom, looking for the drugs, threatening to burn up everything if she didn't obey him.

That was the beginning for me. I had never seen any woman attacked by the man she was living with, who she shared a bed with, had children with. I was in shock.

He was not intimidated when I photographed him in the privacy of his own home. I grabbed his arm and asked him what he was doing, and he flung me off and said he was teaching her a lesson.... From that point on I felt an obligation to learn about domestic violence.

  I live in people's homes quite a bit, I live in the homes of men who have had a history of violence but have been through the batterers' re-education program. However, you never feel safe sleeping in homes with people like this, who've had a history of violence. So I'm always filled with trepidation, and I sleep with one eye on the door at all times.

Q: From that first time, you had to be aware that you were putting yourself in physical danger almost as great as the spouses'.

Yes. But I could leave the next day. I guess that I thought as many women do in these situations, He won't kill me. He won't pull the trigger on that gun. We were lucky. I didn't realize how dangerous it was.

I knew that my greatest weapon was my camera. And I knew that if I didn't have a picture, no one would ever believe that this was going on.... But no matter what he says, I have the proof.

Donna Ferrato is a photojournalist whose intimate portraits of domestic violence have appeared in many major magazines and newspapers, winning her an award from the International Women's Media Foundation.

Part IX

Review Essay

26

The Death of a Reporter

D. D. Guttenplan

The Salonika Bay Murder
Edmund Keeley. Princeton, 1989.

The Polk Conspiracy
Kati Marton. Farrar, Straus and Giroux, 1990.

Who Killed George Polk?
Elias Vlanton. Temple, 1996.

On March 12, 1947, President Harry Truman addressed a joint session of Congress. His topic was the civil war then raging in Greece, the result, said Truman, of "Soviet efforts to destroy the political independence and territorial integrity of Greece." In rhetoric that would echo from Athens to Saigon, the president said the U.S. should "make full use of its political, economic, and, if necessary, military power in such manner as may be found most effective to prevent Greece from falling under the domination of the USSR."

Nine months later, *Harper's* magazine ran a progress report on what had become known as the Truman Doctrine. Headlined "Greece Puts U.S. to the Test," the article, by a rising young journalist named George Polk Jr., declared U.S. efforts a failure. "The present official American policy has nurtured [a] military monster," Polk found. "If American assistance is terminated," he warned, the Greek Army, "the single properly functioning organ of the Greek government," would be "unleashed upon a country unable to feed her people, furnish her material needs, or meet her daily expenses." The result: a dictatorship, either rightist or Communist. "On the basis of likely return," Polk concluded, "the

$300,000,000 American aid program, as it now stands, is a poor invest-
ment. It is either vastly too much or vastly too little."

Polk was no radical. But he was an independent thinker, in a time
when independent thinking was becoming a dangerous indulgence—
especially among journalists. Polk knew the risks. That same month, in
a letter resigning from *Newsweek* over the magazine's editorial slant,
he wrote: "I've wrestled for weeks with my convictions versus what I
regard as Newsweek's lack of objectivity.... I don't like the innuen-
does that seem to me to have become Newsweek's stock in trade.... Of
course, I know that a letter like this could draw charges that I'm a
Communist, but I'll stand on my past, present and future work to refute
such a possible charge."

Polk was also not a reckless man. Though Truman's Federal Loyalty
Security Program was less than a year old—and Joseph McCarthy still
an obscure junior senator—the witch-hunt was well under way. A man
with a "questionable" background could lose his job over such a charge.
As a decorated veteran of Guadalcanal whose ancestors included a president of the United States, perhaps George Polk figured he could take
the heat. Besides, his principal employers at CBS had only the highest
praise for their chief Middle East correspondent.

Indeed, if things had turned out differently—if he had been a less
aggressive reporter or Greece had been less dependent on American
aid—a generation of Americans might well have grown up tuning in to
"The CBS Evening News with George Polk." He had the pedigree: a
descendant of President James K. Polk and churchman-turned-Confed-
erate major-general Leonidas Polk, he had graduated from the Virginia
Military Institute and been awarded the Purple Heart. Just as important, at least at CBS, Polk was one of Ed Murrow's protégés, hired right
after the war into a charmed circle of correspondents that included Eric
Sevareid, Charles Collingwood and William Shirer. He also had the
looks; Howard K. Smith described his Texas-born colleague as "a blond
Erroll Flynn." And he had the experience, writing for the *Shanghai
Evening Post* and the *New York Herald Tribune* before joining CBS.
Finally, like any really good reporter, George Polk had a kind of bulldog tenacity that won't let go of a story. It was the tenacity that probably killed him.

On May 16, 1948, a man's body was found floating in the waters of
Salonika Bay. There was a single bullet hole in the back of his head,
and his hands and feet were bound with thick rope. On one wrist was a
watch stopped at 12:20; on the other, a white metal I.D. bracelet with

the name George Polk. Polk had been missing for about a week, and when the police searched his hotel room they'd found a letter to Murrow saying he hoped to make contact with the Communists who were waging a guerrilla war against the American-backed Greek government.

The discovery of Polk's body presented the Greeks—and their American patrons—with an enormous political problem. For this was no ordinary murder. Instead, the young CBS correspondent had become, in I.F. Stone's phrase, "the first journalistic victim of the Cold War."

Before World War II, Greek politics alternated between Royalist and Republican parties, punctuated by right-wing dictatorships. During the Nazi occupation the King, a relative of the British royal family, fled to Cairo. The brunt of resistance to the Nazis was born by the Communist-led partisan army ELAS (People's National Army of Liberation), which became the most powerful political force in Greece after the Germans fled the country near the end of the war. ELAS fought the first round of the civil war with the Security Battalions—a collaborationist force established by the Germans—and then came into conflict with the British Army, which, at Winston Churchill's behest, was energetically trying to organize an anti-communist coalition to restore the King to his throne.

In December 1944, Polk covered the Dekemvriana—the massacre of protesters that sparked off the war's second round—for the *New York Herald Tribune*. Polk's story blasting Britain's role in the conflict quoted a U.S. congressman who charged the Greek police with firing on "unarmed men, women and children who were attempting to demonstrate peacefully against the Greek government's unfair edicts." Polk's reports from Athens for CBS in 1946 noted "the roundup of persons even vaguely suspected of not approving the government and not loving the king."

In February 1947 the British government informed the U.S. it could no longer afford the Greek campaign, and on Truman's urging America took over as chief bulwark, bankroll and baby-sitter for a series of very shaky Greek governments whose main—sometimes only—virtue was their fervent anti-communism. In a letter to his family, Polk described our new clients as "fascist and below the belt in every way." His copy was more measured, but Polk's view that "Greek government 'outright injustice' has converted more Greeks than Moscow's agents could" did not make him popular with either the State Department or Athens. A year later, he was dead.

The official version of Polk's death—that he'd been killed on orders from the Greek Communist Party—was accepted by both the U.S. government and by Polk's employers at CBS. But not by I.F. Stone, the muckraking radical journalist.

Stone knew the official version was "a whitewash"; he'd said as much in print at the time. In 1971, at a ceremony where he was given the George Polk Award, Stone was bothered by a previous speaker's "antiseptic reference to him being killed on his way to interview an insurgent leader. The fact is that Greece was our first Vietnam,...and the crushing of the revolt then stands in a lineal relationship to the present [Greek] dictatorship. George Polk was...murdered by the Greek police who tried to frame the murder and blame it on the Left, although George was one of the only friends the Left had."

He ended his remarks with a suggestion: "One of these days, somebody ought to do the story of George Polk in all its implications and its relationship to the agony of Greece under our imperialist oppression."

Elias Vlanton's *Who Killed George Polk?* is the latest of three recent attempts to do exactly that. Like his predecessors, Vlanton offers only pieces of a puzzle set at the hazardous crossroads of Cold War politics and corporate journalism. Taken together, though, these books open a window on a crucial, if sordid, episode in American history.

As whitewashes go, the official version of George Polk's murder wasn't particularly convincing. There was an alleged perpetrator: Gregory Staktopoulos, the Salonika stringer for Reuters. There was a confession—or rather, confessions, since Staktopoulos confessed to several different scenarios culminating in Polk's murder. And since Staktopoulos was clearly somebody's dupe, there were the evil masterminds—two officials of the Greek Communist Party. Staktopoulos claimed they asked him to come along as a translator, lured Polk into a rowboat with the promise of transport to the guerrillas' mountain headquarters, persuaded Polk to allow himself to be blindfolded and bound hand and foot, and then shot him in the back of the head and dumped his body overboard.

The press conference announcing Staktopoulos's arrest and confession also detailed a motive: "Polk's murder was planned...in order to throw the blame of the murder to the Right, thus to defame Greece abroad and to stop the application of the Marshall plan to Greece...and also to frustrate the military aid to Greece." Staktopoulos was picked up in August; he confessed in October. He'd spent the intervening weeks confined to a cell at security police headquarters. "Two months in solitary confinement may make a man tell the truth," wrote I.F. Stone in an October 1948 column commenting on the arrest. "Or it may make him say anything his jailers want him to say. This is one of the reasons for the right of habeas corpus. That right does not exist in Greece."

Stone had no way of knowing that one of the two Communist leaders accused of murdering Polk had himself been killed by artillery fire more than a month before Polk's death, nor that, as later emerged, Staktopoulos had been tortured for days at a time while his mother and sisters were held in nearby cells. Yet he was the only American reporter to publicly question the official line.

CBS sent two correspondents to monitor the Greek police investigation; both of them endorsed the Staktopoulos solution. Walter Lippmann, who'd been a mentor to Polk and had recommended him for a Nieman Fellowship at Harvard shortly before his death, organized the Overseas Writers Special Committee to Inquire into the Murder of George Polk. Though their number included William Paley of CBS, James Reston of the *New York Times,* columnist Marquis Childs and *Newsweek's* Ernest Lindley—in Lippmann's phrase, "men whose profession it is to have few illusions"—the Lippmann committee detected nothing amiss in Staktopoulos's fanciful account.

There are many possible explanations for this credulity, from conspiracy to cowardice. My own sense is that fear of the consequences of pursuing leads that pointed to the right should not be underrated.

Other journalists, whatever their motives, looked at the case and turned away. Howard K. Smith, CBS's chief European correspondent, cabled the State Department his opinion that it was "highly unlikely" Polk had been killed by left-wing forces. But Smith, who asked the network to let him head up its investigation into the murder (and was refused) never spoke up to criticize the Lippmann committee's report.

By the time the Lippmann report came out in July 1952, the Royal Hellenic Air Force was no longer dropping American napalm on Greek partisans—we'd "won" Greece and were busy in Korea. With the Cold War at a fast boil, asking impertinent questions about America's triumph in the Balkans was a bad career move. But while fear—or, in Walter Lippmann's case, a view of high statecraft that placed *raison d'état* above the truth about a colleague's murder—kept the U.S. press quiet, in Greece the truth was beginning to leak out.

In 1956 Staktopoulos managed to smuggle a series of letters asserting his innocence past his jailers. Four years after his trial and conviction he was still being held at security police headquarters—ostensibly for his own protection. A number of Greek journalists now interested themselves in "I Ipothesi Polk"—the Polk Affair—which had become a national conundrum, a milder version of American disputations over the Rosenbergs or Alger Hiss. And with each new disclosure, the whitewash got a little shabbier—a process interrupted, but not ended, by the Colonel's dictatorship that began in 1967.

When the Junta fell in 1974, the official solution was doomed. In 1976 a detailed account of Staktopoulos' interrogation and fabricated confession was published in Greece; the following year *More* magazine ran an article alerting American readers to the fact that George Polk's murder was still unsolved.

The demise of the official theory left three questions to be answered: Who killed George Polk? Why was he killed? And how did so many leading lights of the American press come to endorse the cover-up despite what I.F. Stone called "advance warnings enough to have set a cub reporter on guard"?

Though all three books address themselves to this last—and in some ways most significant—question, the most thorough account of how the American and Greek governments (again in Stone's words) made accomplices out of a "bunch of journalistic stuffed shirts" comes in Edmund Keeley's *The Salonika Bay Murder*. Keeley, a professor at Princeton and distinguished translator of modern Greek poetry, published in 1989 what was essentially a scholarly account of the existing Greek literature on the Polk Affair illuminated by his own considerable knowledge of the diplomatic context and supported by recently declassified State Department archives on the case. The son and brother of American envoys to Greece, Keeley manages to turn the dry cablese of State Department communiqués into the flesh and sinew of imperial administration.

Keeley argues that from the moment the Lippmann committee engaged William "Wild Bill" Donovan as counsel and chief investigator, their efforts to solve Polk's murder—or pressure the Greek government to do so—were subordinated to a Cold War definition of the national interest. The former head of the OSS may well have seemed an inspired choice to Lippmann, whose first act as chairman was to request a meeting with Secretary of State Marshall.

Donovan's whole investigation, as Keeley says, "demonstrated an unusual commitment to cooperative enterprise between the executive branch of the government and the Fourth Estate." But such close collaboration had a price. Donovan, who apparently knew very little about Greece, appointed a Greek-American Air Force officer, Colonel James Kellis, as his own man in Salonika. During the German occupation, Kellis had been an OSS liaison officer with ELAS.

Kellis had the knowledge and the contacts to conduct a thorough investigation and had begun to do so when the American *chargé d'affaires* in Athens sent a secret cable to the secretary of state: "Embassy believes sooner Kellis removed from scene the better." The Air Force discovered a pressing need for Kellis, who was recalled after less than six weeks in Greece.

With Kellis safely out of the way, Donovan and the Greek security police were able to arrive at a mutually satisfactory conclusion. "An arrest is desired," Donovan told the Greeks. An arrest was made.

The signal virtue of Keeley's account—his scholarly caution—is also the book's main defect. One of the more interesting subplots in the Polk Affair, for example, concerns the role of one Randoll Coate. An information officer at the British Embassy who may also have been a spy, Coate appears to have been the last non-Greek to see Polk alive and was transferred to Oslo immediately after Polk disappeared. Over the years Greek accounts have made much of the Coate connection, but after summarizing them Keeley says simply "without further evidence…it seems only reasonable to give him the benefit of the doubt." No bulldog Keeley, who gives only the briefest glance at the two police reporters' questions, Who killed Polk and why? On the other hand, it is unlikely Professor Keeley will ever have grounds to regret a sentence of his book.

The same cannot be said for his two successors, Kati Marton and Elias Vlanton. Marton's *The Polk Conspiracy* was published to considerable fanfare in 1990. Although part of the attraction was doubtless due to Marton's status as a journalistic insider, the better part of the excitement was due to Marton's claim to have figured out "who ordered the assassination of George Polk—and why."

Marton argued that Polk was indeed murdered by the Greek right, specifically a Piraeus-based thug named Michael Kourtessis acting at the behest of Foreign Minister Constantine Tsaldaris. Polk apparently stumbled upon evidence that Tsaldaris had sent $25,000 out of Greece to an account at Chase Manhattan, a violation of currency control laws that, if exposed, would have seriously embarrassed the Greek and American governments. Polk confronted Tsaldaris, vowing "This will finish you!" and thereby sealed his fate.

There are many problems with Marton's account, including a sometimes breathless writing style and an occasional willingness to attribute thoughts and dialogue: "The Acropolis Hill seemed suspended in the soft early-morning light. The marble columns shone pink and apricot, and Polk thought he had never seen anything so breathtaking." Such acts of divination are made worse by footnotes that are, by scholarly standards, fairly shoddy.

These are real faults, but as a reporter Marton is a bulldog in the best George Polk tradition. She thanks Theodore White for background on Shanghai in the 1930s; novelist Dan Jenkins filled her in on Fort Worth, Texas, Polk's hometown. But Marton also found Randoll Coate and interviewed him in London. She conducted over a hundred other interviews, as well as turning up numerous archival finds that seem to have eluded Keeley. Finally, but crucially, Marton reached someone who gave her the secret personal files of James Kellis. These apparently provided the leads for her resolution of the case.

How convincing is she? That is the question put most elegantly by Ronald Steel, who in a review of Marton's book pointed to "the gap between what is known, what can be reasonably surmised, and what can be persuasively demonstrated." Here two separate sets of problems emerge, as catalogued, at book length, by Elias Vlanton.

Vlanton notes that Marton's blow-by-blow reconstruction of Polk's murder is at variance with some inconvenient facts. For example, Marton says Kourtessis tried to contact Polk in March and April, but the fight with Tsaldaris didn't happen until May 3. Also, she has Kourtessis travel to Salonika between May 4 and May 6. But when Polk left Athens on May 7, he was on his way to the northern Greek city of Kavalla and only changed his plans when flooding closed the airport there. (This point was also raised by Ronald Steel.) And Marton's account of how Polk's body was smuggled out of his hotel in a laundry basket—then dragged across several busy streets without anyone noticing—strains belief.

Yet some of these apparent inconsistencies may well be answerable. Kourtessis, for instance, may have been keeping tabs on Polk as a matter of general principle. And the solution Vlanton offers—that Polk was killed by petty black marketeers to protect their smuggling operation—is based on supposition at least as flimsy as anything in Marton's book.

The second set of difficulties surrounding *The Polk Conspiracy* is Marton's extensive reliance on sources that are not publicly available.

Even for journalists, the use of unattributed sources is increasingly frowned on. Historians have their own rules—and are no better than anyone else when it comes to keeping them. Still, once a work has been safely published the general practice is to make all sources available to other scholars. Marton's lack of deference to scholarly fashion can be inferred from her footnotes. And her unwillingness to furnish Vlanton further rope to try to hang her is entirely understandable. But with her journalistic triumph secure, perhaps she should now make the Kellis files and other documentary evidence uncovered by her enterprise part of the public record.

While Marton's version of exactly *who* killed George Polk may be in need of revision, her judgment as to *why* he was killed seems by far the most persuasive case yet made.

As for Vlanton, as co-author of the 1977 *More* article, he's been at work on the Polk mystery longer than anyone else. Yet the result of his labors, *Who Killed George Polk?*, was only published this year—after both Marton's book and a "60 Minutes" report based on her book. His criticism of her work, therefore, is hardly disinterested. Also, though Vlanton's footnotes are a model of scholarly utility, his command of the basic facts of the story is less than wholly convincing.

On the simple question of whether Polk was blindfolded, for example, Marton, citing the coroner's report, argues there never was a blindfold. Her logic is complicated, but fairly compelling. Vlanton, who never passes up a chance to correct the record elsewhere, here simply asserts the body was blindfolded. Vlanton also theorizes Polk's letter to Murrow was forged by his killers, who supposedly stole a file of his correspondence to mimic his style but somehow neglected to make off with his typewriter, which they left out on the table.

Yet for all the shortcomings in his account of the murder, Vlanton provides the thickest description we have so far of the Greek context—and of American naiveté. His depiction of Greek aristocrats, U.S. bureaucrats and kleptocrats of both nationalities all scratching one another's backs in the name of anti-communism goes a long way to explain why we may never know who killed George Polk. And ironically it is Vlanton who, despite all his efforts to discredit a political motive for Polk's murder, provides the most eloquent summary of exactly what was at stake politically:

> At a time when public support for U.S. aid to Greece was essential to the success of the aid program, the most immediate effect of George Polk's death was to silence a critical voice reporting the reality of the Truman Doctrine. With U.S. aid flowing into Greece at the rate of $1 million a day, the Greek government and U.S. officials sought to prevent critical press coverage on a wide range of issues, including economic reconstruction, political rights and the Greek military. If American journalists reported that U.S. aid was being used to prop up a repressive, corrupt and wasteful government, domestic support for the aid program would have vanished.

Vlanton also offers us the cautionary tales of two journalists who didn't go along with the spirit of the times. One was John Donovan, Polk's opposite number at NBC. Fired by the network a few days after refusing an NBC official's demand that he resign from an independent committee investigating Polk's death, Donovan became obsessed with the case; he even filed a complaint with the FCC charging all three networks with suppressing evidence of a cover-up. In Vlanton's phrase, Donovan "never again worked in mainstream journalism."

Neither did William Price, a cousin of Polk's and a reporter for the *New York Daily News*. He lost his job at the *News* after refusing, on First Amendment grounds, to answer a Senate subcommittee's questions about his political views. Price drove a school bus, worked as a playground attendant and did interviews for a market research company to support himself. If he'd lived on into the '50s, would Polk's career have been so different?

George Polk was a troublemaker, and in that sense he was an embodiment of the best traditions of his profession. It was Polk's fate to be a casualty of the Cold War, and to have been murdered at a time when expediency was prized over courage. In a more confident era, Polk probably wouldn't have been killed. At the very least, his murder might have prompted a renewed determination to carry on his work, as happened after the assassination of *Arizona Republic* reporter Don Bolles. Sam Spade, in Dashiell Hammett's *The Maltese Falcon,* put it as well as anyone: "When a man's partner is killed he's supposed to do something about it."

Far from using their influence to demand justice, the response of Polk's colleagues, said I.F. Stone, would "provide journalism school with a model lesson in how to be a willing sucker instead of a real reporter." The Cold War is over; "our side" has won. But there are still plenty of takers for those lessons.

If George Polk's life and death have any meaning now, it is in the words he typed on that winter's day in 1947: "I think a man or a publication should resist the impulse to drift with popular pressure just because it's easy."

As long as his story inspires one or two journalists to resist—to continue to make trouble—then George Polk will not have died in vain.

D. D. Guttenplan, a 1993–94 Media Studies Center fellow and a former New York Newsday *reporter, is currently writing a biography of I. F. Stone.*

For Further Reading

Alliance of Independent Journalists. *Banning 1994*. Jakarta: 1994.

Anderson, Terry A. *Den of Lions: Memoirs of Seven Years*. New York: Crown, 1993.

Anton, Ted. *Eros, Magic and the Murder of Professor Culianu*. Chicago: Northwestern University Press, 1996.

Arnett, Peter. *Live from the Battlefield: From Vietnam to Baghdad: 35 Years in the World's War Zones*. New York: Simon & Schuster, 1994.

Arnot, Charles. *Don't Kill the Messenger: The Tragic Story of Welles Hangen and Other Journalistic Combat Victims*. New York: Vantage Press, 1994.

Article 19. *In the Shadow of Buendia: The Mass Media and Censorship in Mexico*. London: 1989.

Committee to Protect Journalists. *Attacks on the Press: An Annual Worldwide Survey by the Committee to Protect Journalists* (published in March).

Duzan, Maria Jimena. *Death Beat: A Colombian Journalists Life Inside the Drug Wars*. Translated by Peter Eisner. New York: Harper Collins, 1994.

Essential Liberty: First Amendment Battles for a Free Press. New York: Columbia University Graduate School of Journalism, 1992.

For Rushdie: Essays by Arab and Muslim Writers in Defense of Free Speech. New York: George Braziller Inc., 1994.

Forer, Lois G. *A Chilling Effect: The Mounting Threat of Libel and Invasion of Privacy Actions to the First Amendment*. New York: Norton, 1987.

Gjelten, Tom. *Sarajevo Daily: A City and Its Newspaper Under Siege*. New York: HarperCollins, 1995.

Headley, Lake. *Loud and Clear*. New York: Henry Holt, 1990.

Inglehart, Louis E. *Press Freedoms: A Descriptive Calendar of Concepts, Interpretations, Events and Court Actions from 4000 B.C. to the Present*. New York: Greenwood Press, 1987.

Nerone, John. *Violence Against the Press: Policing the Public Sphere in U.S. History*. New York: Oxford University Press, 1994.

The New York Public Library. *Censorship: 500 Years of Conflict*. New York: 1984.

Niazi, Zamir. *The Press Under Siege*. Karachi, Pakistan: Karachi Press Club, 1992.

Ogbondah, Chris W. *Military Regimes and the Press in Nigeria, 1966-1993: Human Rights and National Development*. Lanham, Md.: University Press of America, 1994.

Ostroff, Roberta. *Fire in the Wind: The Life of Dickey Chapelle*. New York: Ballantine Books, 1992.

Padhy, Krushna Singh. *Battle for Freedom of the Press in India*. Delhi, India: Academic Foundation, 1991.

Reporters Sans Frontières Annual Report: *Freedom of the Press Throughout the World*. London: John Libbey.

Schwartz, Eric. *Still Confined: Journalists in "Re-Education" Camps and Prisons in Vietnam*. Washington: Asia Watch Committee. New York: Committee to Protect Journalists, 1987.

Simon, Bob. *Forty Days*. New York: Putnam, 1992.

Simon, Paul. *Freedom's Champion: Elijah Lovejoy*. Carbondale, Ill.: Southern Illinois University Press, 1994.

Stenbuck, Jack, ed. *Typewriter Battalion: Dramatic Front-line Dispatches from World War II*. New York: William Morrow, 1995.

Trotta, Liz. *Fighting for Air: In the Trenches with Television News*. New York: Simon & Schuster, 1991.

Wells-Barnett, Ida B. *Crusade for Justice: The Autobiography of Ida B. Wells*. Edited by Alfreda M. Duster. Chicago: University of Chicago Press, 1970.

Wendland, Michael F. *The Arizona Project: How a Team of Investigative Reporters Got Revenge on Deadline*. Kansas City: Sheed, Andrews and McMeel, 1978.

Index

175